Recollections of a Southern Daughter

Edited by Lucinda H. MacKethan

RECOLLECTIONS OF A

Southern Daughter

A Memoir by

Cornelia Jones Pond

OF LIBERTY COUNTY

The University of Georgia Press   Athens and London

© 1998 by the University of Georgia Press
Athens, Georgia 30602
All rights reserved
Designed by Sandra Strother Hudson
Set in 11 on 15 Monotype Walbaum by G&S Typesetters, Inc.
Printed and bound by Maple-Vail
The paper in this book meets the guidelines for permanence
and durability of the Committee on Production Guidelines
for Book Longevity of the Council on Library Resources.
Printed in the United States of America

02   01   00   99   98   C   5   4   3   2   1

Library of Congress Cataloging in Publication Data

Pond, Cornelia Jones, 1834–1902.
Recollections of a southern daughter : a memoir by
Cornelia Jones Pond of Liberty County / edited by
Lucinda H. MacKethan.
p.   cm.
Includes bibliographical references.
ISBN 0-8203-2044-7 (alk. paper)
1. Pond, Cornelia Jones, 1834–1902.   2. Liberty County
(Ga.)—Biography.   3. Liberty County (Ga.)—Social life
and customs.   4. Plantation life—Georgia—Liberty
County.   5. Georgia—History—Civil War, 1861–1865—
Personal narratives.   6. United States—History—Civil
War, 1861–1865—Personal narratives, Confederate.
I. MacKethan, Lucinda Hardwick.   II. Title.
F292.L6P68   1998
975.8′73303′092—dc21   98-22321
[b]   CIP

British Library Cataloging in Publication Data available

On the title page: Charles Fraser, *Another View of the Same*
(Ashley Hall). Reproduced by permission of the Gibbes
Museum of Art/Carolina Art Association.

CONTENTS

ACKNOWLEDGMENTS

I am deeply grateful to Mrs. Jo Ann Clark, director of the Midway Museum, and to the Midway Society for their permission to publish this new and complete edition of Pond's recollections. Mrs. Clark has been extremely helpful and generous with all the materials held at the museum. Without the dedicated work of the many people of the Midway community who give their time to the Midway Museum, the history of one of the South's most remarkable church communities would be lost.

My thanks also go to my recently retired colleague, Professor and Associate Dean Michael S. Reynolds, and to the College of Humanities and Social Sciences at North Carolina State University for providing encouragement and financial assistance for travel to archives. I am also grateful to Professor Lester D. Stephens, of the Department of History, University of Georgia, who shared his wealth of knowledge of the LeConte families and William Louis Jones. The staffs of the University of Georgia Libraries in Athens, the Atlanta History Center and Department of Archives, Atlanta, and the Liberty County Clerk of Court's office in Hinesville, Georgia, all provided great assistance. Thanks go also to Louis D. Rubin for his always wise advice and to my daughter, Karen D. MacKethan, for invaluable aid in helping me to transcribe Pond's manuscript. Finally, to Eugenia Barber Esham and her husband, David Esham, I express my gratitude for their friendship and their generosity in sharing with me the Eugenia Jones Bacon Papers, which sparked my first research visits to Liberty County and led me to Cornelia Jones Pond.

INTRODUCTION

The narrative of Cornelia Jones Pond, daughter of a wealthy rice planter, is an unusual memoir that offers an intimate portrait of a southern girl's coming of age in the Old South. Pond began dictating her "recollections," as she called them, to her daughter Anne in 1899, when she was sixty-five years old. Her story begins in 1834, when she was born on her father's extensive plantation, Tekoah, located near the South Newport River inland from the Georgia coast in Liberty County some thirty miles below Savannah. Her narrative stops with the year 1874, when Pond was a forty-one-year-old minister's wife and the mother of four daughters, making her way in a drastically changed postwar South. The memoir encompasses, then, one of the most intriguing and still controversial regions and eras in American history. Moreover, the story comes to us in the gentle, often nostalgic voice of a white southern woman of the slaveholding class, a voice that remains a challenge to interpret, even with all the analytical tools we can now bring to bear on the difficult questions of the time and place she portrays.

Pond's announced purpose in telling her story, close to the end of her life, was simply to give pleasure to her children and grandchildren. Certainly she did not expect to see her memoir published. Thus, as taken down by her daughter, her reflections have the liveliness of a face-to-face conversation with a beloved listener. As we come to read Cornelia Jones Pond's words almost one hundred years after she spoke them, it is with the perception that we are listening in on very personal reminiscences of a woman who did not see herself as exceptional. Her recorded life commands our attention because of her ability to render for us, with striking immediacy and affectionate detail, not only her own personal past but also the huge upheavals of history that she witnessed firsthand.

Pond lived the charmed existence of a belle in one of the wealthiest agricultural counties in the South. Liberty County was home to a unique planter elite, favored descendants of devout Puritans who had arrived in Massachusetts in 1630. Their plantations had been carved out of the Georgia coastal swamplands beginning in the 1750s. The society they established has become one of the most famous antebellum southern communities of American history, in large part through three volumes of the letters of the Charles Colcock Jones family that Robert Manson Myers collected in his monumental work *The Children of Pride* (1972). This collection of letters has become one of our most useful sources of information on southern plantation society. The Presbyterian minister and wealthy rice planter Charles Colcock Jones was known as "Apostle to the

Slaves" for his missionary efforts in Liberty County between 1833 and 1847. *The Children of Pride* relates, through letters written to and from members of his family between 1854 and 1868, the story of everyday lives of the planters of this county, how they thrived and, during the 1860s, how their world was destroyed. Cornelia Jones Pond's family, although not related by blood, were neighbors, fellow church members, and friends of the Charles Colcock Joneses.[1] Many of the experiences that Pond records parallel those depicted in *The Children of Pride*, thus extending our knowledge of the people of this region, their values, their everyday concerns, and the huge national drama that engulfed their families in the years of civil war.

The Jones family into which Cornelia was born in 1834 was, if anything, more prominent than that of Charles Colcock Jones. Her father, William Jones, was a learned and devout as well as a physically energetic man, a well-respected church and civic leader and an unusually knowledgeable plantation manager. His paternal grandparents, Samuel Jones and Rebecca Baker Jones (Ball) (Quarterman), belonged to the first generation of white settlers to come to the fertile Georgia coastland known in colonial times as the Midway District. Samuel Jones, along with his wife's father, William Baker, received some of the earliest land grants made available in the Midway District, giving them hundreds of acres to cultivate. Samuel Jones II, Cornelia's grandfather, gained so much land that he founded the summer retreat of Jonesville, Georgia, providing lots on which his children and neighbors could build gracious homes on high ground safely removed about four miles west of their swampy plantations.

Mary Cornelia Jones, "Nela" as her name is spelled in the text of her recollections, was the third of four children born to

William and Mary Jane Robarts Jones. Growing up in Liberty County, she and her two brothers, Louis and Sam, and one sister, Rosa, were spared no luxury or advantage. Her reminiscences of her early years constitute an idyll of parties, excursions, feasting, churchgoing, and dancing. Fancy bonnets, dolls, a piano, educational opportunities were hers, and when she married, an elaborate trousseau, furniture, a yearly cash allowance, and "servants" to cook and to nurse her babies. All her needs and desires were generously supplied by the man she always called "Father." Cornelia grew up secure and serene in an atmosphere of privilege and luxury. "What a dear, good father I had!" she exclaims.

Yet this pampered, much loved daughter returned, as a young wife and mother, to Liberty County in 1861 in time to witness firsthand her family and neighbors "stripped of everything," as she put it. Her father's beautiful Jonesville home, the home in which Cornelia had been married, was burned, along with the homes of several neighbors. Tekoah was plundered of livestock, foodstuffs, and many valuable possessions when troops attached to Kilpatrick's wing of Sherman's army, fresh from their devastating march eastward from Atlanta, swept through Liberty County in December 1864, destroying everything in their path.

Pond's personal reflections on her life, from her idyllic childhood on the bountiful plantation to her adulthood in an impoverished and socially revolutionized and defeated region, constitute an especially valuable resource for those pursuing an interest in the plantation South in its dramatic midcentury years. The complex relationships between masters and slaves, the role of plantation women in a carefully structured patriarchal society, the responses of the planter class to the monumental reverses wrought by war—all of these are rendered through a somewhat deceptively simple narrative that attentively describes both daily routines and momentous events. Pond speaks without a sense of a public audience to please or to persuade. Certainly she wants to give special emphasis to the things she cherished about her world. Her own family, like the Charles Colcock Joneses, were "Children of Pride," and Pond clearly sees herself as handing on the traditions and values of her class. In doing so she gives us some of the same stereotypes of happy slaves, caring paternal masters, the *good* times "befo' dah wah" that we recognize as staples of the white southern literature that began to be popular during Reconstruction. Such literature, with its racist overtones and blind spots, remains even today dangerously seductive, as the continued popularity of *Gone with the Wind* demonstrates. Pond's account is rarely defensive, and less propagandistic than many penned during her own time and later, partly because her attitudes and responses belonged to a construction of events that was meant for the private sphere of her own family and not for the public arenas. Pond is carrying on a conversation not with critics or historians of the Old South but with those who are familiar with her experiences or those who, she naturally assumes, will grow up to share her point of view.

What did Cornelia Jones Pond want to tell her own descendants, what do her recollections tell us, and what else do we need to know to make some balanced judgments—first about the land, economic assets, and social customs that were so central to the narrator's sense of herself; then about the values of a daughter who revered a "home" that included close to one hundred slaves; and finally, about the resources with which she and her family faced the dramatic changes in identity and status that came with the Civil War? Her world was rich in history, resources, and contradictions, which is what makes her recollections so fascinating for us to listen in on today.

I

LIBERTY COUNTY is located on the Georgia coast below Savannah, an area protected from the Atlantic by the sea islands and crisscrossed by several rivers and tidal creeks. The swamplands a few miles from the coast were, in the eighteenth and nineteenth centuries, ideal for cultivating rice and sea island cotton. Early residents who began to settle on these lands in the 1750s quickly established the first profitable agricultural operations in the Georgia colony. On the political front, the Midway District produced several heroes during the Revolutionary War and two signers of the Declaration of Independence, Lyman Hall and Button Gwinett. The county grew steadily throughout the early nineteenth century, and by 1860, census rolls listed 2,284 whites and 6,083 slaves.

Liberty County was founded both as a religious and as a slave society, and therein lies perhaps its most troubling contradiction. Cornelia Jones Pond's forefathers were dedicated Puritans who had journeyed to Massachusetts from Dorchester, England, in the early seventeenth century to obtain religious freedom. Their quest for wealth and security took them in the 1690s to South Carolina, where they soon could claim some of the largest plantations on the Ashley River. Ironically, these liberty-loving Puritans owned thousands of slaves as well. When they contemplated a move to Georgia, in order to provide even more land for their growing numbers, they waited until 1752, after the colony legalized the importation of

slaves within its borders. Then many of them left their plantations in South Carolina to resettle on the large isolated tracts
along Georgia's southern coastal rivers.[2] By 1760, rice planters
who settled in the Midway area, most of them connected to the
"Dorchester Puritans," owned one-half of the slaves in Georgia, and they began to amass enormous wealth.

The Liberty County planters were staunch patriots during
the Revolution, and after the establishment of the new nation,
they continued to thrive. Through slave labor, they built a society that epitomized the white southern plantation ideal;
however, their particular religious orientation caused them to
fashion a unique version of that ideal. The "Southern Puritans" who settled at Midway before the Revolutionary War
had stayed together since leaving England, and they held uni-
formly to their sect's traditions of worship and conduct. Midway Church, originally a Congregationalist denomination, but
one early affiliated with other southern Presbyterians, domi-
nated the county's social as well as its religious life.[3] This focus had one particularly significant consequence in relation
to the way slave life was managed in Liberty County. Several decades before Charles Colcock Jones began, in the late
1830s, his famous campaign to instruct and direct Liberty
County slaves and slaveholders in their duties as Christians,
Midway Church members had provided financial support for
white ministers and slave "exhorters," as they were sometimes
called, to preach to the slaves. The Reverend Jones's efforts,
which included popular catechisms and guides, intensified the
evangelical spirit among slaveholders. For slaves, the masters'
interest in their spiritual orientation meant community contacts that went far beyond the realm of their daily physical la-
bors. The responsibility for religious welfare that the planters

assumed, undoubtedly with mixed motives, made their owner-
ship of slaves even more fraught than usual with contradictions.
Slaves seem to have been very much aware that, for many masters, the chief advantage of Christian instruction was an in-
crease in the docility and obedience of their chattel.[4]

Midway Church, as Cornelia Jones Pond notes, provided a
unifying center to the lives of many of the county's families,
black and white. For the free, even if they moved miles away
and organized other churches, Midway, the church and its
cemetery, was the defining core of their history. For the en-
slaved, the well-organized program of religious indoctrination
meant that they had more levels of interaction with the white
community, for good or ill, than most slaves. Cornelia's father,
William Jones, was centrally involved, by ancestry as well as
personal endeavor, in the Midway Congregationalist vision.
His great-grandfather, William Baker Sr., had been named the
church's first deacon in 1754; he himself was a Select Man
from 1836 to 1841.[5] The Joneses held to the Midway strictures
on social behavior; they abstained from alcoholic beverages,
and the daughters danced only the quadrilles (except at home,
girls with girls). Sunday for the Joneses and their slaves was ex-
clusively devoted to religious activity—even during the Civil
War, Cornelia reports, the knitting of socks was suspended on
the Sabbath. Her memoir shows that while her family knew
how to live well, they also kept a stern eye on their spiritual
obligations and those of their slaves as well.

The people of Liberty County whom we meet in Pond's narrative reflected the place to which they felt such a heightened
sense of spiritual and social loyalty. Liberty County was fairly
isolated from the outside world. Pond notes the coming of rail
travel to Georgia as a major event of 1849, but until several

railroad lines were completed through the county in the mid-1850s, her own frequent trips between home and Savannah were taken by private carriage or stagecoach. Owing partly to the county's isolation and partly to the strong presence of the church to which so many of the founding settlers of Liberty County belonged, intermarriage among neighboring families was common. Pond was not exaggerating when she said that she was related to almost everyone in the county; her relations included Varnedoes, Cays, LeContes, Quartermans, Ways, Winns, Bacons, and Mallards. No doubt her family's immediate approval of Thomas Goulding Pond as a suitor had something to do with his impeccable Liberty County connections (grandfather Thomas Goulding was Liberty County's first native Presbyterian minister).

Common customs and values among people so closely related would seem a matter of course. Beyond religious practice, defined and closely regulated by Midway Church doctrine, the attention to education was also a remarkable feature of the Liberty County life that Pond's memoir elaborates. These were people for whom schooling from the elementary grades through some sort of college training was a common expectation—for both young men and young women. Beginning with Cornelia's first schoolmaster, Samuel McWhir Varnedoe (called "Ole Mac"), she, along with cousins and other neighboring children, encountered high standards in her educational settings. Liberty County was known throughout the first half of the nineteenth century for the quality and quantity of its schools and for the number of ministers, statesmen, authors, and educators it produced. It is significant that the Jones daughters' education beyond local offerings was deemed a priority. William Jones and his brother Moses Liberty Jones both sent their daughters away from home to some of the earliest academies and colleges for women established in the state of Georgia. William Jones's first choice for Cornelia was Montpelier Institute in Macon, founded by the prominent scholar-minister who was to become the first Episcopal bishop of the diocese of Georgia, the Reverend Stephen Elliott. After a year there, she finished her education at the Methodist Female College in Madison, Georgia, again a school of her father's careful choosing.

II

NEITHER education, marriage, nor travel seduced Cornelia from her first attachment, the plantation home and family that represented her definition of every charm. Until her parents and brothers all finally abandoned their landholdings there in the 1870s, she looked back to Liberty County always as a sacred refuge. The first two parts of her narrative, detailing her childhood and her activities as a young belle, dwell lovingly on every personal aspect of life at Tekoah and Jonesville. Here, too, inescapably, is where Pond also voices the southern patrician view of slavery and thus where we see clearly that she wholeheartedly embraced the white plantation South's favorite illusion—its idea of itself as a familial organization of masters and slaves bound to one another in a mutually sustaining relationship.[6]

As we meet them in her recollections, slaves simply "belong"—from childhood onward trained for special duties within the master's household or beyond it, in the fields. They are carriage drivers, for instance, who take the girls to dances and watch them proudly through porch windows, or seam-stresses who hand-sew silk and lace undergarments for missy's trousseau, or little guardians who walk their young white own-ers to school, carrying the lunch pail, waiting outside to escort them home at the end of the day. (One ominous, even if mi-nor, note, however, stands out when Pond talks of her walks to school—she mentions, only in passing, that she was afraid, during these excursions, of "runaway negroes.") Once Cornelia is grown and married, slaves are shipped to her, as needed—as for example her twelve-year-old maid, Kate, sent to her by train from Liberty County all the way to Tuskegee, Ala-bama, the key to a trunk full of presents tied securely around her neck. Interestingly, Cornelia, as a bored and lonely young bride, teaches Kate to read and write, and Kate, she says, stayed with her until after the war. We can speculate about the intimacy that might have developed between these two, both of them in a sense exiled from the family and privileges they enjoyed back "home" in Liberty County. Pond is silent about whatever feelings of affection or dependency she might have felt for the girl whose companionship must have filled many needs.

Pond has a self-serving view of what motivated the freed-people's behavior after the Civil War finally disrupted most of the bonds between the Jones slaves and their owners. She de-clares that those servants who abandoned their place in the family were "demoralized"; those who kept their place and functions were "faithful." No other explanation seems war-ranted; at least, no other is given. Again we speculate concern-ing what went on among the slaves during the time that the Yankee soldiers were a daily presence on the grounds once controlled by the master. The Jones slaves acted individually, according to what must have been conflicting feelings of loyalty, self-interest, habit, hope, and fear for the future.

When we look to Pond's narrative to answer the question we want to ask of all slaveholders—how could they bear to own and use other human beings and risk, if not perpetrate, the tyrannical abuses of power that are endemic to a slave system— her definition of slavery as a benignly "domestic" institution is the only answer we receive. It is the answer, of course, that Harriet Beecher Stowe turned on its head in her powerfully effective antislavery novel, *Uncle Tom's Cabin* (1851). Pond, in her narrative, never challenges the version of the Old South that the slaveholders crafted to justify their way of life, yet it does not seem to be an issue on which she wants to take much of a stand.

A year before Pond began telling her story to her daughter, Pond's first cousin Eugenia Jones Bacon published a novel of slave life based on memories of her father's (Moses Jones) Liberty County plantation. In Bacon's *Lyddy: A Tale of the Old South* (1898), the title character is a mammy, the children's nurse, whose interactions with her white mistress-narrator (a very thinly disguised version of Eugenia Jones Bacon herself) form the core of the plot. Bacon's post-Reconstruction novel was an effort, as she herself announced in her preface, to redeem the Old South from the antebellum attack that Harriet Beecher Stowe had mounted.[7] As Pond records her memories, she makes a different choice than her cousin. Pond's recollections do not deal with close attachments to her "servants," much less with overt defenses of their owners. Slaves are depicted as colorful, at times humorous, usually affectionate, often indispensable, yet Pond's tone is rather surprisingly detached as she describes her interactions with them—they are simply part of the whole fabric of plantation life. Of course her tone does change, decidedly, when she begins to tell of the "disloyal" slaves who "betrayed" her family by stealing hidden possessions left in their care by her trusting father when the Yankees overtook the county.

As we look at the contours of Cornelia Pond's life up until December 1860, when neighboring state South Carolina seceded, we can gather some useful, if indirectly supplied, evidence about the day-to-day lives of William Jones's "servants." Their existence was regulated and directed by the master, who named them, provided their food and clothing, and decided where and in what capacities they would expend their labor. Religion, we notice, was emphasized for the slaves, who were furnished with their own "praise house," a kind of chapel, on the plantation grounds.[8] Paternalism is the system that Pond describes in her recollections. If she saw or felt anything that might contradict the vision of a world safely and sanely managed by a master who was father to all, she does not reveal it.

Pond writes a script that exalts the planter as patriarch and the plantation as family; however, one of her reminiscences recalls a particularly idyllic family scene involving another famous Liberty County patriarch, Roswell King Jr., a slave owner for whom we have another, far less sympathetic witness—Fanny Kemble. In Kemble's *Journal of a Residence on a Georgia Plantation in 1838–1839*, the famous British actress tells of her brief tour of duty as a plantation mistress on the estate of her husband, Pierce Butler. An ardent abolitionist whose later divorce from Butler caused a huge sensation, Kemble was horrified by the conditions of slave life that she found when she, her husband, and two young daughters briefly resided on his sea island plantations, located off Liberty County's coast. Roswell King, Butler's overseer as well as a wealthy plantation owner himself, was singled out for special condemnation in Kemble's *Journal*. In particular, Kemble notes that King had sired children by his slaves, and she also recounts instances of his cruel punishments of slaves. King's own letters to Butler regarding plantation affairs, as well as other contemporary accounts, tend to corroborate Kemble's stories. Yet when Cornelia Pond visited King's estate on Colonel's Island in 1849, she was enchanted with the "beautiful boatsongs" that the slaves sang as they rowed her company over to the island and the cordiality of the entire King family—Mr. King, his wife, her mother, and several of the King children: "I consider this one of the happiest weeks of my life," Pond reports. She saw, we might add, what she wanted to see.

Pond's account of her family's slaves is limited to the privileged "house" slaves, not the hundreds of slaves who worked in her father's rice and cotton fields. The slaves who served the Jones's personal needs within the home had several kinds of family ties. Pond refers to these people with what might seem to us incredible casualness. "Father, Brother, and his negro boy Tom, and I left for Savannah," she will recall, including this slave in her list of her traveling party as a matter of course. Many of the Jones house slaves had "belonged" to the family for more than one generation; they were often "deeds of gift," presents made on special occasions or provided in wills with some attention to keeping the slaves' own blood families intact. Slave mothers and their children occupied coordinate places: Mum Chloe is the cook, her son Titus the coachman; Mum Phyllis, also a cook, is mother to Nellie, a "beautiful seamstress," whose sister "Feedee" is the chambermaid. When

Cornelia takes her personal maid, Kate, to Savannah, Kate's mother, Belle, is brought up to be the cook. There are families, then, within families in this scheme.

By the master's conscious design, the well-being of black family retainers reflects their owners' bounty. Thus Mrs. Jones, in one of her daughter's recollections, admonishes coachman Titus for not wearing proper footwear when he takes her out to drive, because, she says, "People will think that I do not give you good shoes." [9] Slaves were symbols of the master's status and munificence. To see their "servants" well dressed and happy, with secure families of their own, was to protect the system that provided for the master's own happiness.

Thus, until close to the end of the Civil War, slaves are made to fit seamlessly into Cornelia Pond's vision of "home." Tekoah plantation for her was an icon of order, the symbol of carefully arranged processes that ensured a serene, idyllic pace to life. The design of the plantation house, the layout of extensive gardens, the duties of field hands and cooks, nurses and coachmen, all the way up to master and mistress, were defined with this pace in mind. At the head, master indeed of all he surveyed, was the patriarch—in this case William Jones. The world Cornelia describes is, more than anything else, a patriarchy. Without question William Jones saw himself first and foremost as father and provider. In relation to his daughter, he supervised major issues such as schooling and keeping strict Sabbath practices, yet he was also notably sensitive to small matters, remembering, for instance, to bring Cornelia a very fancy bonnet that she particularly coveted as a little girl. On more than one occasion he took her to Savannah to shop; he directed the buying of her elaborate trousseau; he sent wagonloads of furniture and plantation delicacies to her when, as a young matron, she and Thomas Pond established their first home in the city.

William Jones in the public sphere beyond his family saw himself, and was known by others, as an exemplary plantation manager. While some of his neighbors might be absentee owners, William and his brother Moses Liberty Jones, whose lands adjoined his, were centrally involved in every aspect of the running of their estates. Tekoah and Moses Jones's Green Forest were two of the largest and most profitable in the county.[10] Cornelia makes passing reference to her father's interest in botanical and agricultural experiments; he achieved lasting fame, in fact, by successfully introducing the cultivation of tea on his plantation.[11]

Wealth for the people who were Cornelia Pond's family, friends, and neighbors brought with it obligations to succeed, to meet high standards in relation to the larger society. Pond mentions her frequent contacts with her neighboring cousins the LeContes—father Louis and sons Joseph and John were among the most learned Americans of their time. Her brother Louis (William Louis Jones) studied with Joseph LeConte under Professor Louis Agassiz at Harvard and was a professor at the University of Georgia for most of his adult life.[12] Her brother Sam was a physician, and her husband was a professor of mathematics before he decided to enter the ministry after the Civil War. Her husband's uncle Francis Goulding was a minister and author of a famous book series ("The Young Marooners") for children. After the war, her father left the plantation to publish, with son Louis, the most highly regarded agricultural journal in the South, the *Southern Cultivator*. Pond was related to two United States senators from Liberty County, Alfred Iverson, who served from 1852 until secession, and Augustus O. Bacon, who served from 1894 until his death in 1914.

The Jones family's wealth also meant, despite Puritan strictness, an opulent lifestyle that seems to have been very conspicuously cultivated. Conversing with her daughter more than forty years after the end of the Civil War, Cornelia Pond takes a fond and remarkably well detailed look at her family's possessions and indulgences in antebellum times—the two elegant homes, the fine clothing and furniture, the lavish parties, the well-equipped carriages, the exquisite gardens. We know from Cornelia's descriptions of her dresses and bonnets that she wore clothing designed according to the highest standards of fashion and made out of the most stylish and expensive fabrics.[13] Her most memorable family friends, the John Barnards and the Roswell Kings of Colonel's Island, were two of the most glamorous as well as wealthiest of Liberty County's elite. Her father's high-stepping gray horses, the quality and extent of Cornelia's trousseau, the elegant style of her wedding, held at the family's summer place in Jonesville—every detail is a sign of status, of success, of a patriarchal system working according to plan.

The life of a plantation belle portrayed here follows, in some ways, the rhythm of the seasons: in summer, when the family moved to Jonesville to escape the malarial swamps, life took a more social cast. Likewise, when the young men came home from college in November for their two-month break, the round of parties and the accompanying intensity of courtships increased. The all-day Sunday attendance at Midway Church provided a weekly gathering that was in many ways as much socially as religiously compelling. The women strolled out of the church through groups of men lined up on the front steps, talking and no doubt assessing the feminine parade. Made to be seen, dressed and educated and trained in all the social graces, Cornelia was a reflection of her father's priorities and strengths. She was an ornament, but a functional one, with an important role to play in how the system showed itself to the world.

There is little question that Cornelia's upbringing was designed to ensure just the eventuality that transpired—a union with an acceptable young man of solid means and impeccable family connections. Marriage to a man who was not a planter, but instead a teacher, might have meant some wrenching changes in lifestyle for Cornelia, but we note how her father mitigated these alterations, especially after the Ponds moved to Savannah, by supplying many of their wants directly from the plantation. Thinking of her fashionable home in the city, after her father's bounty had arrived, Cornelia Pond could exclaim, "I felt like a little girl with her doll house, so proud of my new crockery and furniture." Servants imported from Tekoah handled the labor in Savannah just as they had back home in Liberty County.

III

IF THE CIVIL WAR had not intervened in Cornelia Jones Pond's life in a very direct and personal way, it is quite likely that her memoir would not have been created. Her life as she herself seems to have preferred it was for the most part a quiet, unremarkable one. Up until 1864, the closing year of the war, Cornelia had no reason to know that her situation would place her at the center of a social and political revolution. As a young matron in Savannah in the 1850s, she was wholly absorbed in family matters. Her first two daughters were born; her husband made a fine salary at the fashionable public school, Chatham Academy; her Liberty County relatives visited almost constantly. The change in status that seems to have been most important to the Ponds, on the eve of secession, involved religion. She and her husband, after much soul-searching, became attached to a religious denomination that separated them from the Midway Church family when they were baptized and confirmed as communicants of St. John's Episcopal Church.

Pond's memories of political and military events that took place in the early months of the war are dim in comparison to what she remembers of her loss of her year-old daughter Alice, who died of scarlet fever in June 1861. Soon afterward, when Thomas Pond took up the first of several different posts in the Confederate army, Cornelia moved back to her parents' refuge in Liberty County. She remained complacent during the first years of war: "The servants were not demoralized yet," she tells us, "and things moved peacefully along." The challenges of making do without accustomed goods involved ingenuity, yet trying out new kinds of dye for clothing and hats and new ways to make medicines, or mastering the art of weaving on a large loom, provided welcome activity. A "daughter of the Confederacy," Eloise, was born, and there was even a wedding, as sister Rosa married her childhood sweetheart, the dashing cavalry officer Captain Benjamin Screven.

In May 1864, however, Thomas Pond left with Screven to serve the Twentieth Georgia Battalion in Virginia; Cornelia would not see him again until the war was almost concluded the following April. Thomas Goulding Pond fought in some of the bloodiest Confederate battles of the war, the Wilderness campaigns in Virginia. Back in Liberty County, in December 1864, Cornelia, with her parents, sister, sister-in-law, and bedridden brother Sam, watched as Yankees entered the grove at Tekoah. Nothing in her life would ever be the same. The summer home at Jonesville was burned, as were many plantations near Tekoah; almost daily for close to three weeks, Yankee soldiers arrived at the Jones plantation to take whatever they could find.[14]

Cornelia Jones Pond's account of these literally earthshaking events is similar to those written by several of her relatives and neighbors who, like her, were eyewitnesses and, to their own way of thinking, innocent victims of unjustifiable Yankee violence. One effect of General Judson Kilpatrick's foragers was to turn many Liberty Countians into reporters; those who kept journals or later wrote accounts of what they saw and heard include Pond's first cousins Eugenia Jones Bacon and Joseph LeConte, along with several members of the Reverend Charles Colcock Jones family (the Reverend Jones's wife, Mary, his daughter Mary Jones Mallard, his son Charles Colcock Jones Jr., and his son-in-law Robert Quarterman Mallard). All of these individuals wrote eventually published accounts of plantation life. Most were stirred to write by the destruction wrought at their homes during the last month of 1864.

It is particularly useful to pair Pond's account of the war with Joseph LeConte's posthumously published narrative, 'Ware Sherman (1937), and an account culled from Mary Sharpe Jones's and Mary Jones Mallard's Civil War diaries, entitled Yankees A'Coming, published in 1959. All three works focus on families who were living on their Liberty County plantations, or in LeConte's case, one who had just returned to the county to rescue his daughter and other female family members, when units from Kilpatrick's cavalry arrived in mid-December. Their versions of the events that took place in Liberty County in late December intersect at many points. The planters who had stayed in their Liberty County homes crossed paths with their friends, trading similar stories of atrocities and hairbreadth escapes. The white citizens all were desperately involved in trying to save what they could of their valuable belongings and in dealing with what was for them the most shocking loss of all—the loss of their ability to trust the slaves who, though they had always been numbered among other "belongings," now took advantage, in surprising numbers, of the opportunity to announce their self-ownership. As Mum Chloe warned Mrs. Jones: "The world don't stand like it been."

The fact that Cornelia's father was one of the few men of health and vigor, despite his age, who was on hand during the time of the Union army invasion made the Joneses' experience a little less grim than most. Liberty County during the war was, like most of the plantation South, increasingly a world of women and slaves, having on both sides to try to adjust to one another in a drastically new order.[15] But at Tekoah, William Jones remained forcefully in charge, although one of his most trusted slaves betrayed to other slaves the whereabouts of some of the valuables that the master had taken great pains to hide. Both the Joseph LeConte and the Jones-Mallard accounts mention "Uncle William": when Joseph LeConte leaves the county with his female dependents, he takes what he knows to be a wise course in securing William Jones's promise to manage his estates. Mary Sharpe Jones mentions the comforting visit of an "Uncle William," almost certainly William Jones, during the time that the Yankees were foraging on their estates.

That a figure of the stature of William Jones would be mentioned in these recollections is not surprising, but another figure who appears in all three of these white autobiographical
narratives is an unusual hero—a slave, Marlborough Jones,
who was owned by Cornelia Pond's close friend and first cousin Laura Jones Camp. Although Marlborough appears only
briefly, and early, in Pond's memoir, Joseph LeConte and Mary
Sharpe Jones identify him by name or owner and tell stories of
how they depended on him to help them get through enemy
lines during the Yankees' occupation of Liberty County. Marlborough is also the slave hero of Eugenia Jones Bacon's Civil
War novel *Lyddy*, in which the author/narrator tells of how
Marlborough returned her brother Randal Jones's body home
to Liberty County for burial in the fall of 1864, after accompanying him to the battlefields in Virginia.[16] Thus four different Liberty County writers document not only the world of the
masters but, in one case at least, the very dramatic existence of
a slave.

For Cornelia Jones Pond and her family, the events of December 1864 signaled the end of a way of life. Her father
mourned that he had personally lost the work of forty years.
Like the Charles Colcock Joneses, Cornelia's family found that
their slaves responded in divergent ways to the changes, some
showing great bravery in protecting their vulnerable masters
and others showing equal courage, although owners did not
interpret it as such, in taking on new roles involving self-
interest and a bold expression of freedom. Pond's words about
the newly freed slaves—"Now for the first time we began to
know fear of those who formerly had been our protectors"—
say volumes about her situation and her blindness. Never, before the war, would she have admitted that she needed her

slaves to protect her, and one wonders at her new recognition of fear—Liberty County had never been immune, in the years before the war, to the fear of slave uprisings.[17]

The Joneses met changes with resilience, whatever their inner qualms. By the spring of 1866 Cornelia's father and her husband, who had survived bloody battles and a long, solitary trek home, were making a good crop, paying wages to the freedpeople to do housework and to labor in the fields.[18] Symbolic of the resolve to move ahead, to forge new lives, was a quilting party, including a fine dinner for the invited ladies, that Cornelia managed to pull together in Jonesville in the fall of 1866: "We were getting quite prosperous now," she says, somewhat tongue in cheek, of their ample but plain repast.

By February of the following year, however, Cornelia Jones Pond and her husband and children had "left the dear old county for good," and the unthinkable, that her own father would give up Tekoah, followed not long after. Letters of the Joneses' neighbor Jane LeConte Harden to her brother John, regarding William Jones's attempts to manage his and Joseph LeConte's plantations from late 1865 to 1867, are indicative of the struggles that most planters faced in the postwar years. Writing in December 1865, Jane Harden sends William Jones's grim message: "Uncle Wm said I must say to you that your negroes had left you very little of anything." She also reports the indignity that the Joneses had earlier experienced firsthand: "Now they are continually having white men arrested and carried to the Freeman's court in Sav. [Savannah]."[19] Cornelia Jones Pond tells how her father, in the spring of 1867, moved permanently to Athens, Georgia, where he and son Louis, who had returned to Athens in 1866 to resume his teaching at the newly reopened University of Georgia, purchased the *Southern*

Cultivator and closed the book forever on their own attempts to manage plantations.[20]

Cornelia Jones Pond's account of her family's history in the ten years following the end of the war concentrates primarily on her husband's decision to enter the ministry as an Episcopal prelate, on the births of two more daughters, who perhaps in some ways consoled her for the two who had died just before and just after the war (Alice in 1861 and Mary Cornelia in 1865), and on her own struggles with debilitating rheumatoid arthritis. Thomas Pond, who with Cornelia had taken the dramatic step, early in 1861, of becoming an Episcopalian, gladly picked up on his spiritual quest where he had left off when the war took him away from St. John's Church in Savannah in 1861. After surviving several fierce engagements as a cavalry officer with the Twentieth Georgia Battalion in Virginia (brother-in-law Benjamin Screven was shot through the windpipe at Hawes Shop; his wife's first cousin Randal Jones later died of wounds received at Trevellian Station, where Pond's horse was killed), he seems gladly to have returned to a quiet life, responding to a call to the ministry in 1870. His decision took his family to Alabama, where for the next four years he accepted several different church-related positions. Cornelia Jones Pond's dictation to her daughter ends with her poignantly remembering that in 1874, struggling with the disease that had totally crippled her, she feared that she would soon be buried in an Alabama churchyard.

Lucy Pond, Cornelia Pond's oldest daughter, in 1925 added some notes to her mother's account to bring the Ponds' family history up to date. We hear that Cornelia indeed did not die but was able to move in 1875 back to her beloved Georgia, when her husband accepted a call to St. Paul's Episcopal Church in

Albany. In that year, the Ponds were finally blessed with a boy, after the births of six girls, five of them born to the father's exclamation, "*another* darling daughter." One last move in 1887, connected with Mr. Pond's ill health, took the family to Mt. Airy, Georgia, where Pond supervised several small northern mountain missions.[21] Interestingly, among these was an unorganized mission at Toccoa, and thus a familiar name re-entered Cornelia's life; William Jones, for reasons unknown, had given his plantation the name "Tekoah," a variant of the name of the northeast Georgia mountain village.

IV

FROM HER MEMORIES Cornelia Jones Pond constructed the vivid image of a southern daughter, wife, and mother whose own fate was determined by the fate of the white slaveholding South. In many respects, she was an image maker all of her life. Forty years after her entrance into society as a young belle, she could recall down to the last grosgrain ribbon how men and women of her class dressed, how they conducted their church services, what they ate at parties. It was her duty to know these things, to weave and spin a kind of litany to the accoutrements that defined and sustained a very highly regulated, subtly ritualized style of life. Pond seldom discusses politics or public life, but she demonstrates that she herself, in her dress and demeanor, and above all in her perfect domesticity, embraced definitions of race, gender, and class that were, at heart, deeply political in their causes and effects.

Any attempt to assess Pond's purposes in fashioning the kind of memoir she undertook must acknowledge both what we do and do not know of the conditions involved in her presentation of events. Her story was dictated during the last three years of her life, under circumstances of transcription that we are unable to verify. When she and Anne Pond Bacon began the project, Anne had been recently widowed (in 1897) and had moved to her mother's and unmarried sister Lucy's home in Mt. Airy, Georgia. Cornelia was blind, as a result of glaucoma. The bond between the two widows, teller and listener, mother and daughter, is clear from the conversational tone, the naturalness of the diction, the care with which every word is carefully captured.

It is difficult to compare Pond's memoir with many of the other published diaries, journals, and memoirs that were penned by white southern women of the same period. Most of the published ones are much more self-consciously literary or political in their tone—that, for instance, of Mary Boykin Chestnutt (*Civil War Diary*, first published posthumously in 1905), or two that have closer regional and personal ties to Pond's: Emma LeConte's *When the World Ended* (first published in 1957) and Frances Butler Leigh's *Ten Years on a Georgia Plantation* (1883).[22] Importantly, LeConte (later Furman) and Leigh, like Mary Chestnutt but unlike Cornelia Pond, did not spend all of their formative years on a plantation closely supervised by the planter-father himself. Although there are many reasons for differences in the way principles are voiced among these works, the stability of Pond's life as a plantation daughter up through the Civil War was an essential factor in how she modulated the voice that presents her life.

Pond's particular interpretation of her southern principles caused her to see herself, and to conduct herself, as a background figure. The girl and woman she presents to us is not a decision maker, or a questioner, or a debater, although, significantly, she does recapture her horror at hearing that Lincoln's presidency would bring war. She does not seem to have believed that any abstract political principle could be valued against the risk of losing home and husband. Importantly, as well, it turns out that Cornelia's happiness did not depend on her being a member of the slaveholding class. Memories of her father's material losses bring anguish, descriptions of the Yankee soldiers' behavior arouse expressions of angry disdain even after so many years, and the slaves' defections are recalled with a tone of bitter shock, but we can sense in this narrator an indomitable but also flexible spirit that contained much simple practicality. Within a year of the war's end, she could say, "It seemed that we had started life anew." Her story of the slave cook, Mum Chloe, is instructive: during the Yankee invasion, Chloe at first refused to help her masters, so that when later she wanted to return to her place, William Jones angrily came down and kicked her out of the kitchen. In days to follow, however, the Jones women watched longingly as Chloe passed by. The last we hear is that Chloe has been "received back into favor." Father's principles do not hold forever against household needs, especially for women with children to feed, women who had never learned how to cook.

The postwar years, as Pond remembers them, were happy ones, with her own growing family living in cities such as Columbus and Mobile that were themselves beginning to thrive in a New South. Yet wherever she went, and as long as she lived, Cornelia Jones Pond associated herself with the image of daughter—in other words, as a dutiful, obedient, helpful, and dependent adjunct to the men in her life. Indeed, this is the role that the patriarchal plantation South demanded, the one that her father instilled, and the one modeled consistently by the figure of her usually silent, shadowy mother. We also take note that Pond was telling her story to her own daughter, close to the beginning of a century that would, in its first years, mount effective challenges to the purely domestic ideal of womanhood.

Cornelia Jones Pond's version of history, then, is marked by her self-conception, her relation to her audience, and her time of life—the urge to preserve her personal interpretation of the past is a motive connected to all three elements. A century later, we might suspect her serenity of tone or frown on her emphasis on what seem to us at best trivial, at worst materialistic concerns. Her voice seems an odd amalgamation of selfishness and selflessness, combining as it does such a complacent acceptance of all the comforts of caste and class with such self-effacement and personal modesty. Throughout, there is an appreciation of beauty and of family that no disheartening events ever diminish. *Recollections of a Southern Daughter* attests to the many complexities of the world it describes. The narrative offered in a woman's quiet yet confident voice contributes to our knowledge not only of southern history but of how many different voices are necessary for any understanding of that history. Cornelia Jones Pond, a planter's daughter of Liberty County, kept her memories amazingly intact for almost half a century. In a region famous for its love of storytelling, she and her daughter relished the sharing of a story that speaks compellingly to new listeners now, one hundred years later.

NOTES

1. See the appendix, "The Liberty County Family of Cornelia Jones Pond," for a listing of many of the people who were shared ac-

quaintances of these two Jones families. William Jones's plantation, Tekoah, was located in southern Liberty County, approximately eight miles south of Midway Church, along the border of what is now McIntosh County. The Charles Colcock Joneses owned three plantations in the county. In 1854, Charles Colcock Jones's daughter, writing to a friend, warned: "Do write soon, and be particular in directing to Father's care; for since Laura Jones and family have returned, several mistakes have been made with our letters" (see *Children of Pride* [New Haven: Yale University Press, 1972], 1:139). Laura Clifford Jones was Cornelia's close friend and William Jones's niece. Her plantation, Green Forest, adjoined Tekoah.

2. See George A. Rogers and R. Frank Saunders Jr., "The Dorchester Connection: The Genesis of the Midway Settlement," in *Swamp Water and Wiregrass: Historical Sketches of Coastal Georgia* (Macon: Mercer University Press, 1984).

3. For histories of Midway Church, see James Stacy, *History of Midway Church* (Newnan, Ga.: S.W. Murray, 1951), and Robert Manson Myers, prologue to *Children of Pride*.

4. See Stacy, *History of Midway Church*, 208–244, and Erskine Clarke, *Wrestlin' Jacob: A Portrait of Religion in the Old South* (Atlanta: John Knox Press, 1979).

5. See the lists of deacons and Select Men in Stacy's appendix in *History of Midway Church*, 329–38.

6. See Ann Firor Scott, "Women's Perspective on the Patriarchy in the 1850's," in *Half Sisters of History: Southern Women and the American Past* (Durham, N.C.: Duke University Press, 1994), and Elizabeth Fox-Genovese, *Within the Plantation Household: Black and White Women of the Old South* (Chapel Hill: University of North Carolina Press, 1988).

7. Eugenia Jones Bacon's *Lyddy: A Tale of the Old South* was published by Continental Publishing Company in 1898. The third daughter of Cornelia's uncle Moses Liberty Jones, Bacon (1840–1920) wrote of some of the same occurrences as Pond in her memoir.

Both tell, for instance, of the trials of Bacon's sisters, Laura Jones Camp and Leonora Jones McConnell (Stacy), during Kilpatrick's occupation of the county in December 1864. Pond and Bacon do not make any references to each other. Their lives took different paths after the war; however, it is somewhat striking that Pond does not remark on the death of her beloved Uncle Moses, in 1851, one year following his wife's death in childbirth. William Jones was executor of his brother's estate, and Cornelia's close friend Laura, the oldest of Moses Jones's children, became, in effect, the guardian of her seven orphaned siblings.

8. The "Praise House" was a common feature of many rice plantations, a place where slaves often conducted their own worship services, although, as Pond notes, many slaves also attended Midway Church with their owners. For studies of slave religion in this region of the South, see Charles Joyner, *Remember Me: Slave Life in Coastal Georgia* (Atlanta: Georgia Historical Collection, 1989), and Clarke, *Wrestlin' Jacob.*

9. The concern for slaves' shoes, as well as their problems getting shoes that fit, seems to have been widespread. In *Chronicles of Chicora Wood* (Atlanta: Cherokee Publishing, 1922), to give just one other instance, Elizabeth Allston Pringle writes, "The hardest thing of all was the shoes. . . . Darkies have a great dislike of big feet, so many of them were tempted to send too short a measure" (when they were given a stick and told to mark the length of their feet so that shoes could be made); "and then what suppressed groans and lamentations when the new shoes were tried on" (155).

10. Moses L. Jones and William Jones were two of the wealthiest slaveholders of Liberty County. George A. Rogers and R. Frank Saunders Jr. report that, according to 1850 census records, 70 percent of the county's 362 families owned slaves, but only 7 percent owned more than 50. The 1850 census records list Moses Jones as owning 110 slaves and William Jones as owning 82. Cornelia mentions some

150 slaves milling in the yard of Tekoah on the day after Union soldiers ransacked the plantation house and grounds. See "Black Dirt and High Ground: Agriculture in Nineteenth-Century Liberty County, Georgia," in *Swamp Water and Wiregrass*, 157; also Robert Long Groover, *Sweet Land of Liberty: A History of Liberty County, Georgia* (Hinesville, Ga.: WH Wolfe, 1987), 29–38.

11. Stacy, in *History of Midway Church*, 310–13, tells the story of William Jones's cultivation of tea plants and of how, after the war, a Mr. John Jackson of Scotland attempted to make tea growing a profitable venture on the Jones plantation, part of which he rented. Stacy includes an interesting sketch of a house that Jackson apparently built on stilts on the old Tekoah land, believing that a house built above the "malarial stratum" would be safe from that disease. Groover, in *Sweet Land of Liberty*, reported that as late as 1900 "the old tea fields near Riceboro could still be found" (58).

12. See Lester D. Stephens, "William Louis Jones and the Advancement of Scientific Agriculture in the South during the Era of Reconstruction," *Georgia Journal of Science* 49 (1991): 72–80.

13. Cornelia's preference for silks reflects both wealth and international style; likewise, the hoop skirt and as many as six "stiffly starched" underskirts, as well as the low cut of her party gowns, attest to her close attention to changing fashion trends. See Penelope Byrde, *Nineteenth Century Fashion* (London: B. T. Batsford, 1992).

14. For two discussions of the depredations of Kilpatrick's cavalry in Liberty County, from two different points of view, see George A. Rogers and R. Frank Saunders Jr., "The Scourge of Sherman's Men in Liberty County, Georgia," in *Swamp Water and Wiregrass*, 61–72, and Edmund L. Drago, "How Sherman's March through Georgia Affected the Slaves," *Georgia Historical Quarterly* 17 (1973): 361–75.

15. For an in-depth analysis of life on the home front for southern women, black and white, during the Civil War, see Drew Gilpin

Faust, *Mothers of Invention: Women of the Slaveholding South in the American Civil War* (Chapel Hill: University of North Carolina Press, 1996).

16. In addition to the literary records of Marlborough, there is, remarkably, an ambrotype taken of him in Confederate uniform, with this inscription on the back: "Marlboro the—faithful slave— who protected the women of the family while their husbands were in service—the Civil War. He wears the Confederate uniform." This ambrotype is on display at the Museum of the Confederacy in Richmond. It was donated by a descendant of Laura Jones Camp.

17. For descriptions of slave uprisings and other forms of resistance on rice plantations in South Carolina and Georgia, see Julia Floyd Smith, *Slavery and Rice Culture in Low Country Georgia, 1750–1860* (Knoxville: University of Tennessee Press, 1985).

18. Charles Colcock Jones's widow, in a letter to her daughter Mary dated November 17, 1865, remarked on the new relations between masters and slaves: "As I wrote you, Sue [a former slave] had left. She is still at the Boro, and I am told has hired Elizabeth [Sue's daughter] to work at Dr. Samuel Jones's." Dr. Jones was Cornelia Pond's brother. In the same letter, Mary Sharpe Jones writes, in horror: "I understand Dr. Harris and Mr. Varnedoe will rent their lands to the Negroes!" (*Children of Pride*, 3:1308).

19. Three typescripts of letters written by Jane LeConte Harden to John LeConte (dated October 25, 1865; December 13, 1865; and October 30, 1865) are held in the Claude Black Collection at the Hargrette Library of the University of Georgia.

20. For an interesting account of how the *Southern Cultivator* responded to questions of race in the years that it was edited first by both William Jones and Louis Jones and later solely by Louis, see Stephens, "William Louis Jones and the Advancement of Scientific Agriculture," 76–78.

21. Pond's work in the mountain missions is briefly referenced in Henry Thomas Malone's *The Episcopal Church in Georgia, 1733–*

1957 (Atlanta: Protestant Episcopal Church in the Diocese of Atlanta, 1960), 131–32.

22. Emma LeConte was the daughter of Cornelia's cousin Joseph LeConte, and Frances Butler Leigh was the daughter of Pierce Mease Butler, who owned the plantations of Butler's Island below the Jones's residence; both of these women were close in age to Cornelia Pond and, like her, had deep attachments to their slaveholding fathers. Emma tells of witnessing the burning of Columbia by Sherman's forces while her father was in Liberty County, trying to rescue younger daughter Sallie; Frances Butler Leigh tells of journeying with her father back to their plantations after the war ended, to begin a ten-year, ultimately only partially successful project of reclamation. For whatever reasons, these two memoir-type works contain much stronger opinions on slavery, the war, white supremacy, and the wrongs perpetrated by the Yankee government and army than Cornelia Jones Pond's does. Other Civil War memoirs dealing with experiences that relate to Pond's are Eliza Frances Andrews's *The War-Time Journal of a Georgia Girl, 1864–65* (New York: D. Appleton, 1908), Elizabeth Allston Pringle's *Chronicles of Chicora Wood* (New York: Macmillan, 1922), and *A Woman Rice Planter* (New York: Macmillan, 1913), and the privately printed *Louisa* (1995), by Elizabeth Bowne, a novel that tells the Liberty County–based experiences of Bowne's ancestor Louisa Varnedoe, the daughter of Leander Varnedoe, during December 1864 (copy available at the Midway County Museum).

A NOTE ON THE TEXT

*C*ornelia Jones Pond's memoir exists in a handwritten manuscript, 208 unbound sheets, held at the Midway Church Museum, Midway, Georgia. In the last years of her life, Pond was blind from glaucoma and confined to a wheelchair by rheumatism, but her voice comes through to us with great clarity and vigor. According to her opening sentence and her daughter Lucy's closing comments, Mrs. Pond began sharing her wonderfully vivid and detailed "recollections" with her daughter Anne Pond Bacon (Zeigler) at her home in Mt. Airy, Georgia, beginning in 1899, and she had completed her narration by the time of her death three years later, in 1902. Some parts of some pages are damaged and consequently difficult to read, but the handwriting is remarkably clear and legible. The generally good condition of the text allows us to present essentially the whole transcription.

After Cornelia Jones Pond's death, the manuscript seems to have been left in the care of the oldest daughter, Lucy Pond. In 1925 Lucy wrote: "Our dear mother dictated her recollections of her life this far to Anne, and said that I knew the rest and could add it if she did not, so I shall endeavor to tell of the remainder of her life, although I cannot hope to do it in the bright interesting way that she would have told it." Lucy Pond's fourteen-page narrative follows the dictated one in the Midway holding. In an afterword to Cornelia Jones Pond's text, I have quoted the opening comments of Lucy Pond's brief account of the last two decades of her mother's life.

The Midway text is untitled and contains no paragraph breaks or chapter headings. The titles and divisions that I have chosen reflect the themes and the flow of Pond's thinking about her story. I have divided the account into the five major periods of Pond's life as she herself visualized it: her childhood, her years as a young belle, her early married life, her experience of the huge calamity of the Civil War, and her growing family's adjustments in the ten years following the war's end. My editing of the Midway text consists of providing these five divisions in addition to paragraph breaks to make the whole more readable. I have also regularized capitalization and punctuation, using the practice of the manuscript wherever it is generally consistent (including the lack of capitals for "yankee" and "negro"). The spelling and wording follow those of the Midway text; in the few places where it is obvious that a word or letter is missing or where one is totally illegible, I have provided the best guess in brackets. Cornelia Pond's expression, and her daughter's written transcription, contain almost no faltering in style or grammar. Both women, we can tell, were gifted users of language.

The Midway Society, which owns the Midway text, has generously granted permission for this edition. The society also authorized a limited edition (five hundred copies) of Pond's recollections, prepared by Josephine Bacon Martin and privately printed in Hinesville, Georgia, in 1983. Martin titled the portion of the text that she edited "Life on a Liberty County Plantation: The Journal of Cornelia Jones Pond," and she included some sketches drawn by Anne Lee Haynes. Martin was a longtime resident and historian of Liberty County, very active in the creation of the Midway Museum, which opened in 1959, and the author of a pamphlet, "Midway Georgia in History and Legend, 1752–1867."

At the beginning of "Life on a Liberty County Plantation," Martin reproduces a copy of a handwritten letter indicating that Pond's text "was presented to the Midway Association by the great-nephew of the writer, Claude Wright Mitchell." Mitchell was the grandson of Dr. Samuel John Jones, Cornelia Pond's beloved younger brother, who died in Thomasville, Georgia, in 1889. How Claude Mitchell obtained the manuscript is not explained. At the end of her edition, Martin includes a note from M. (Marian) Varnedoe Kumar, dated February 15, 1954, which claims that "the above is a verbatim copy of the original." How Marian Varnedoe Kumar knew of the manuscript is also not explained in Martin's edition. The Varnedoes and the William Joneses were relatives and owned adjoining plantations in Liberty County in antebellum years.

Martin's use of the term "journal" for her edition of Pond's recollections is misleading, given that Pond dictated her memories to her daughter over no longer than a three-year period when she was in her late sixties. In addition, the Martin edition is not itself in fact "verbatim" or complete. Several key

portions of the Midway text were omitted, including the stories of Mum Chloe, of activities at Midway Church, and of
Cornelia's visit with the Roswell Kings on Colonel's Island. In
some places Martin changed the phrasing of sentences or mis-
copied names of people or places. In a few instances Martin's
wording differs substantively from the original Midway text.
However, in one respect, her edition has been very valuable.
Unfortunately, two pages (page 10 and page 47) of the handwritten manuscript are missing from the Midway text. However, they do appear in Martin's edition, so for these two pages
I rely on Martin's text; I have noted these pages in this edition.

Recollections of a Southern Daughter

Recollections of my life,

written to give pleasure

to my children and grandchildren.

Begun October 27th, 1899,

Mt. Airy, Georgia.

A PLANTATION CHILDHOOD

"The world don't stand like it been."

I was born on my father's plantation in Liberty County, Georgia, on March 25, 1834, at seven o'clock in the morning, being Tuesday in Holy Week. My parents were William Jones and Mary Jane Robarts, both natives of Liberty County, Georgia. They were married May 15th, 1823, at the plantation of her widowed mother, Mrs. Elizabeth Robarts, he being twenty-one years and she in her seventeenth year. He took his bride to his plantation which he named Tekoah, and there they lived for more than forty years, until after the Civil War, spending their winters there and the summers in Jonesville, a village four miles distant. This village was named for his father, Samuel Jones, who owned all the adjacent lands for miles around. He gave lots to his friends and children upon which to build, and hence a village sprang up which became the summer home of many of the planters. Jonesville was considered healthy, being on the "pine barrens." The plantations were on the swamps. It was my father's custom to move from Tekoah every May to Jonesville and return the last week of October. I was baptized in old Midway Church by the Reverend Robert Quarterman, when an infant.

My earliest recollection of our plantation home is a house of two stories, two large rooms below and two above, with lower and upper halls between, and with two "shed rooms" opening on a back piazza. There was a wide front piazza fronting on a pretty flower garden in the form of a semi-circle. The house was situated in a large grove filled with beautiful trees of native growth: live oaks, hickory, cedars, holly, pecans, and persimmons. Upon many the wild yellow jessamine grew and formed beautiful festoons of yellow flowers in the early spring. The gray moss also hung in festoons from the live oaks. Two beautiful large magnolia grandiflora trees were to the right of the house on the side as you drove up. They bloomed beautifully in the spring and perfumed the air. Four large live oaks were in the back yard that were planted by my father before I was born. In the flower garden was the magnolia fuscata, or "banana shrub," having been bought by Father from a florist in New Haven, Connecticut. There were also camellias, roses, violets, hyacinths, narcissi, and many others. The grove was surrounded by a fence, forming a semi-circle in front. I suppose it was several acres in all.

My nurse was a negro girl named Annie, who is still living in Liberty County. An incident occurred before I can remember, which has often been told me, which came near taking my life. My father came home one day on horseback, jumped off, and the coachman took the horse. He and my nurse, wanting to give me a ride, hitched my little carriage to him in some way. The horse, Grimes, became frightened and began to run, hitting the carriage against a tree and throwing me out unhurt. Father and Mother, hearing the noise, ran out and met my nurse bringing me in, blue in the face and breathless. As soon as I could speak I said, "Horsey, horsey." I think I was about eighteen months old. Cousin John Burton says he remembers me as a little blue-eyed, auburn-haired girl with loose curls flowing around my head. I have no recollection when I learned to read. Mother taught me my letters on the "Southern Presbyterian," a paper still published. I was the fourth daughter and the fifth child. Two of my sisters, Matilda and Louisa, died before my birth, leaving me with one brother, Louis, seven years older than myself, and one sister, Rosa, nearly five years older than I. They are living at this writing.

In August, 1834, my parents, their three children (I was a baby five months old), the coachman George, and Annie, my nurse, went in their carriage with Miller and Grimes, the horses, through the country to visit my aunt, Mrs. "Renchie" (Amarintha) Burton, who with her husband and children lived on their plantation near St. Mary's, Georgia. The trip occupied several days. They crossed the Altamaha River on a flat and I think the Satilla River too. This was my first journey.

One day in January, 1838, I was told that I had a little brother, who was afterward my much-loved, little play-mate, named Samuel John after his two grandfathers. When Sam and I were little children, Mother used to leave us at home at the plantation on very cold Sundays in the care of "Mum Willoughby," a much-loved and trusted servant belonging to my father. A happy day we always had. When Mother would return, we would follow "Mum Willoughby" to the gate begging her not to leave us. She would good-humouredly say, "Honah (you all) go back, honah do me nuff today." I used to call her "Mum Illerby." This woman was an honest, humble Christian and highly respected. I have often heard Father say he would trust anything he had in her care. She died in 1853, the summer I was married, mourned by us all. After she got too old to cook, Father put her in charge of the young negro children whose parents were at work in the fields. She kept them in a large one-room house with a chimney at each end. This house was called by the negroes "the praise house," because they had weekly prayer-meetings there. She was assisted by the older sisters and brothers of the children. She had a general oversight of them all. Before dismissing them in the afternoons, she would make them stand in a line and repeat the Lord's Prayer after her. It was my delight as a child to hear their "Our Farrer chart in Heaven, Hallud be Dy name" etc. Sister and I used to go there after having been gone all day to the services at Midway Church, and teach the negroes little and big their catechism and begin reading the Bible to them—a Sunday School.

[following is missing (page 10) from Midway text; it appears as page 7 of Martin edition]

When I was five years old I was sent to school to the Academy in Jonesville. My teacher was Mr. Samuel McWhir Varnedoe. He was a very fat man and very severe, using the rod constantly. One day during the first summer my grandmother Jones was coming to spend the day with Mother; I wanted to stay at home but Mother made my nurse Annie take me to school. I cried all the way and on reaching the door of the schoolhouse, my teacher inquired the cause of my behavior. On being told, he slapped my face, took me up in his arms and carried me the full length of the house (about forty feet) and set me upon a high desk which was used by the ministers as a pulpit [Midway text resumes] before the church was built. He scolded me very much which increased my great fear of him, which amounted to terror. He was a good teacher though, a graduate of Franklin College, the University of Georgia. He advanced the children rapidly.

I do not remember when I learned my tables in arithmetic. During the winter the same scholars and teacher occupied a schoolhouse one mile from my father's plantation. I did not commence to go there until I was seven. My brother Louis and sister Rosa and I used to take our little tin bucket of lunch and go to school every day except Saturday and Sunday of course, walking a mile and returning at four o'clock in the afternoon. We had a recess at twelve, of a half hour, to eat our lunch. We only had the month of December for a vacation. I was advanced very rapidly. When I was eleven years of age, I was through arithmetic and algebra and was in geometry. I also began the study of the Latin language at that age. At twelve I was in trigonometry. I was considered a good speller and reader and received a prize for standing up last in a spelling match that fall of 1842. All the school was in this Dictionary class except the little beginners. The prize was a book of fairy tales bound in red, of which I was very proud and read and reread.

At another examination I stood up last, and my Uncle Moses Jones took me up in his arms, kissed me, and promised me a book. It was "Rollo's Vacation," one of the Rollo Books. This I eagerly read, as I did everything I could find. The first book my father gave me was "Masterman Ready," by Captain Marryat. It was bound in green cloth, and I thought it beautiful. Among the books in my father's library suitable to my age were "Robinson Crusoe," "Pilgrims' Progress," and "The Looking Glass," full of beautiful stories and wood-cuts. The books were not filled with pretty pictures like children's books now. My mother used to read "The Looking Glass" when she was a little girl.

Among my classmates was my cousin, Laura Jones, who was two years my senior. We were devoted to one another. She had an exceptionally fine character and bright mind, and it was my ambition not to let her surpass me in anything. She was a good mathematician and linguist, and I studied hard to keep up with her. My mother was very ambitious, instilling into our minds the importance of a good education. She would hear me recite all my lessons before starting to school. It was a mixed school of boys and girls of the county. Nearly all of the boys were sent to college at the age of sixteen or seventeen, and many have become prominent men. Many of the girls went to boarding school well prepared by their thorough schoolmaster. Every October we had a public examination, closing with a spelling match.

We nicknamed our teacher "Ole Mac." He was very severe. It was his habit to pull our ears and pinch the backs of necks and arms and switch us in our hands and over our shoulders if we had imperfect lessons, or make us stand in the floor. I was terribly afraid of him and have trembled in his presence after I was a grown lady. He would open and close his school with extempore prayer. Often have I seen him breathless, after giving one of his boys a severe whipping, clasp his hands over his breast and close his eyes, and dismiss the school with prayer. Once when I was a very little girl, he shut my class up in the schoolhouse and sent the other children home, we thought, leaving us there to spend the night. When everything was silent and all gone, we screamed at the top of our voices. After about a quarter of an hour had passed, Ole Mac returned and gave us our freedom. The others had not gone and left us, but we had been made to believe they had.

He had very white, large teeth which he would grin and grit at the children when they made mistakes. He rode Old Pleasant, a sorrel mare, to school to the winter schoolhouse two miles from his home. He was so fat he had to mount his horse from a stump. When Ole Mac rode by our house it was the signal for us to hurry off to school. We tried to be there ahead of him. Occasionally, he would go in his buggy, and then he would often offer to take me home, and I would hate it and feel so ill at ease. Sometimes we would wake up and find the rain pouring down and we would think we would have a holiday. But often about nine o'clock the sun would come out, and then we would have to take our books and buckets and hurry off to school. These rains became known as "Ole Mac" rains, and so I call them to this day. We had to go to school regularly unless we told Mother that we had sore throat. She was very afraid of that. Sam used to get many a holiday by developing a case, having to swallow lots of soda water as a penalty.

After Brother and Sister went off to school, Brother to Franklin College in January, 1843, and Sister to a private school in Macon in 1845, I had to go to school alone. My mother used to send a negro boy Paul, about my own age, the son of our cook Mum Phyllis, with me to take my bucket of lunch and to "keep the cows off" as she used to say. I used to be afraid of runaway negroes. Paul used to come for me by four o'clock in the afternoon to accompany me home. In rainy weather the buggy was sent for us. After awhile Sam was old enough to go with me, and we used to take our turn at carrying the bucket. We trudged together for three winters along that Sandy Run road. This schoolhouse was one large room with a chimney at each end. The boys were required to gather the wood and make the fires. They also had to go out and gather the switches. Many a time I have seen Ole Mac standing with his back to the fire smoothing the knots off the switches which grew plentifully around in the woods. There was a well nearby with an old-fashioned sweep. The boys had to draw the water and water Ole Mac's horse too, as well as their own.

My first sweetheart was a pretty, brown-eyed boy about my age, a schoolmate named Fleming Law, a son of the Reverend Josiah Law, a Baptist minister. His brother Samuel, two years older, was Laura's sweetheart, and we used to have many confidences about them. In after years whenever we would meet we would refer to that attachment. One day his uncle, Mr. Peter Fleming, told him that if he would tell him the name of his sweetheart, he would give him a peck of sweet potatoes, of which he was very fond. Fleming with a great effort managed to say "N. J." (Nela Jones). "Eh!" said his uncle, "Your sweetheart is New Jersey." Everybody knew about that little affair. He used to sit in church where he could look at me. Many a time I have caught his brown eyes fastened on me in Jonesville church.

I remember going to two tea parties one summer—one at my pretty friend Julia Cay's and the other at the house of Fleming's mother's, Mrs. Law. Fleming escorted me home from both of these. From another party Augustus Fleming saw me home, and as we got in sight of home, thinking Father and Mother were on the porch, I besought him to go home, saying

I was afraid they would see him. He would not do it. It got out in school, and I would hear "Please, Gus, go back. Do Gus go back." In after years Gus would tease me in the same way. I was so modest and very easily teased.

I must not forget to tell you how the little boys and girls dressed when I was a child. The girls wore short dresses made either low-necked, long or short sleeves, or parodi waist, with full short skirts, with long pantaletts to the ankles, white stockings with black slippers in summer and shoes in winter. We wore cottage bonnets like the grown ladies with a cape in the back tied in front in a large bow of ribbon under the chin. There was a white ruching in the side, next to the face, with artificial flowers in it, trimmed on the outside with ribbon and flowers.

I remember distinctly having been made to wear a leghorn bonnet of Sister's which had been done over and trimmed with dark blue ribbon. I was so ashamed of it that I would pull it off as soon as I got in the pew at church. Father, seeing how much I felt this, promised me a pretty one, and the next fall, 1843, he brought me from Savannah a beautiful pink silk bonnet, trimmed with pink ribbon and gilt buttons, and on the inside, in the ruche, were pink and white rosebuds tied under my chin with pink ribbon tied in a bow with long ends. When this new bonnet came, I took the old leghorn bonnet and put it behind an old, large, heavy hair trunk of Mother's and shoved it against the wall, mashing it flat. On Sunday morning, Mother said I could not wear the silk bonnet because I had no suitable [dress] made yet to wear with it. I had to get the old one out from behind the trunk and try to get it into shape, and had to wear it to the morning service. But in the afternoon, after much begging, I was allowed to wear the pink bonnet to church, looking out of place with my summer dress. I felt "the observed of all observers," so proud was I of it.

In June 1843 my cousin Ann LeConte was married to Dr. Josiah Stephens, at our house in Jonesville. Everyone in Liberty County was invited. I was nine years old, and so little I could not see the bride for the crowd. Uncle Varnedoe lifted me up in his arms during the ceremony so I could see the bridal party. There was an elegant supper. This was the first wedding I ever attended.

I do not remember to have had but two dolls, an alabaster one given me by Father, and a lovely wax one brought me by Sister when she returned from her first visit to Savannah. She had real curly brown hair and brown eyes. She was dressed in a white swiss muslin dress over pink cambric, with a pink sash. One day I thought she was cold and put her before the fire and her beautiful face became melted and marred. Cousin Louisa Jones Bacon gave me a little tea set made of white wood decorated with pink flowers. She was Father's niece and the mother of Senator A. O. Bacon. Mother gave me a speckled hen once and told me to name it after the young queen of England, Victoria. I think this was 1841. Father gave me a cow and I sold her for $5.00, and with $3.50 I bought me a string of red coral beads. Father bought them in Savannah for me.

When eleven years of age Father took me to Savannah, my first visit to a city. Sister went with us on her way to school in Macon. We traveled in a large red stage coach, drawn by four horses a distance of about thirty-five miles. It took the most of the day. I remember the smell of the coal smoke as we entered the city. Father gave me $5.00 to spend as I pleased. I bought some colored wools and white perforated paper and different patterns to work bookmarks, needle books, etc. I went to the theater with Cousins John and Josephine LeConte and saw "The Lady of Lyons" acted. I enjoyed the sights of the city very much but was glad to get back to the country. On this trip Father bought a handsome pair of iron gray carriage horses named Altof and Buck. They were the carriage horses from that time till 1856. They were so spirited that Mother was very much afraid of them. I learned to knit lace about this time; Mother taught me. After returning from school in the afternoon, I used to knit lace and insertion and ornament my pantalett.

In Walthourville there used to be a May party every first of May. Sister, Laura, and I used to attend. I generally wore a white swiss dress, low-neck and short sleeves, with pink or blue sash and a wreath of artificial flowers on my head. I used to visit our friends Harriet and Claudia Quarterman. Once Harriet was Queen of the May—a lovely one. After witnessing the coronation of the queen on a beautifully decorated throne on "the green," the boys offered us their arms to take us to the table inside the Academy where delightful refreshments were served. Afterwards we danced; negro fiddlers furnished the music. We danced "the contra dance" and quadrilles—no round dancing. We only waltzed and danced the polka at home with girls. All the village people and county people attend the May parties. It was an annual gathering.

My first recollection of a church was the old Midway Church. The first ministers I remember were the Reverend Robert Quarterman, my father's uncle, and Rev. I.S.K. Axson. The church, as I first remember it, had three doors, one to the north, south, and west. The high pulpit was on the east side. A wide aisle from the north door to the south door, and one from the west door to the pulpit—those aisles crossed, you see. There were galleries on three sides, held up by large, ornamental pillars. There was a belfry and bell. Old Daddy Simon (in green spectacles), belonging to Uncle Robert Quarterman, the pastor, used to ring it. He used to ring and peep down from the gallery to see when the minister entered. As soon as he saw him, he stopped. It used to amuse me to watch him. The pews were very high-backed and had doors. Little children were hidden in them.

I remember the solemnity of "Sacrament Sundays" which occurred only four times a year, the fourth Sunday in every three months, November, February, May, and August. Long tables, two feet wide, extended the full length of the aisles, covered with white linen table cloths, and long benches placed along the sides on which the communicants sat. "The holy table" in front of the pulpit, covered with a spotless linen cloth, held the solid silver service, consisting of a large flagon, four chalices, and four silver baskets with handles over top. After a long service in which there was a sermon of more than an hour, the minister would come down from the pulpit and bless the bread and wine and make a solemn address, and invite the communicants to take their seats at the tables or in front pews during the singing of a hymn. Four elders would go up to the table and the minister would hand them each a basket with the bread. One of them would pass it to him first, then two would go up through the galleries to give it to the negro communicants, and two passed it to the white communicants below. Then he would give each one of them a chalice containing the wine, and the same ceremony was gone through with. My parents were both communicants and this was a very solemn occasion to me, for I felt there was a great difference between us.

The choir was in the gallery across from the pulpit. When

I was a little girl Father was the tenor voice in the choir. He had a very sweet voice too. There was no carpet in this church, no cushions in pews, no stove. We were not expected to be comfortable! No talking or laughing or eating were allowed. Around the church were small houses with chimneys. These houses were called "tents," except the one occupied by the minister and his family which was called "the vestry." Each family would drive up to its own tent, the horses hitched in the woods by the coachman, and the babies and nurses left in the warm tents during the service. A recess about one o'clock, and the congregation lunched in their tents, often inviting their friends to join them. The carriage driver would pass the refreshments around. After lunch we would often walk around the graveyard and visit the graves of our ancestors. This was across the road from the church on the west side, surrounded by a solid, high brick wall. It was filled with beautiful, large live oaks draped in moss. My ancestors as far back as 1752 are buried there.

A second service, shorter than the morning, was held in the afternoon. At the close of each service it was the custom of the gentlemen and boys to go out first, leaving the ladies in the church to greet one another. The gentlemen collected around the church doors and the ladies and girls had to run the gauntlet of all those eyes as they came out. After adieux were made each family entered its carriage and drove home; ours was eight miles distant. Nothing kept us at home but sickness or a very hard rain. If one was absent from church, inquiries were made as to whether he or she were sick. We always enjoyed the nice hot supper which was always earlier. We spent the evenings singing sacred tunes, led by Father and Mother. Both had sweet and true voices.

In the summer of 1849, alterations were made in the church.

The north and west doors were closed and the pulpit was put at the north side and all the pews made to face it. Father's pew was on the east side then. The gallery at north side was put on east side. In the church at Jonesville, the Bible, the chandelier ($50.00) and the lamps on high stands on the pulpit were presented by my grandmother, Mrs. Mary Way Jones, widow of Samuel Jones. These churches were Congregational and had Presbyterian ministers.

Grandmother Jones lived in Jonesville during the summer months with her son, my uncle Moses Jones. It was only during these months that she could attend church. She was too feeble to go to Midway from his plantation eight miles distant. I remember her riding to church in her little low buggy built especially for her and drawn by the carriage driver Marlborough. She would sit by the side of the pulpit to the left in her rocking-chair which Marlborough had previously brought over. As a little child I was impressed by the great respect shown her by everyone, and especially by the minister, who always spoke to her first after descending from the high pulpit. Well I remember her in her black silk dress with a large white kerchief crossed over her breast and a black drawn silk bonnet, with her white tarleton cap showing in front, and white tarleton bow and wide strings tied under her chin.

She was a very pious, good woman, much beloved by her children, and much respected by all. Her mother's people, the Winns, came from Virginia, and she always told us we were related to General Washington, although we never asked how. She died in November 1845 of pneumonia at Uncle Moses' plantation Green Forest. She was in her seventy-eighth year. I went to her funeral. She left Mother as a present, her faithful servant Nellie, whom she had raised from a little girl and whom she had taught to be a beautiful seamstress. She was an excellent Christian woman and remained in our family until she was emancipated. She continued faithful to us after that, taking material to her house and preparing meals for us secretly after the others had deserted us.

The first cook I remember was "Mum Phyllis," Nellie's mother. She cooked for twenty-five years until her death in 1863 before she was freed. She was a very fine cook. She baked my wedding cakes that were made at home and was a splendid meat cook. I must tell you about "Mum Chloe." She was given Father by his father when she was a little girl and mother taught her to be a fine laundress, seamstress, and cook, and she took Mum Phyllis's place after her death. She used to amuse us children by the big words of her own making. Her son, Titus, was the carriage driver for years. One day, upon Mother's inquiring why he was wearing such shabby shoes when he was going to take her out driving, saying "People will think that I do not give you good shoes," he replied, "Yes miss, I got a better pair, but dey no cairn to consarn deyself 'bout my foot."

Chloe was faithful until demoralized by Sherman's army when she left the kitchen. Upon Mother's asking her why she had not been able to help her like Nellie, she replied, "Humph, de wull yew stan like e bin" ("The world don't stand like it been"), showing that she realized the great change that had come between master and servant. But after the army left and the other negroes went back to work in the spring on shares, she came back to the kitchen to resume her work and ran up early to my room where some of the kitchen utensils had been brought, saying, "Miss Nela, way de kittle, way de pots; Lemme go git brekfus!" She went into the deserted kitchen and began working. I went downstairs and told Father, and he went to the kitchen and told her to leave; he did not wish her to work for him anymore as she had been so unfaithful. It was a great disappointment to us when we would see her going to the fields with the hands; we could not but regret that Father had not taken her back. "Fedee," Nellie's sister, was our chambermaid since I was a little child, and filled that place until the War. Her name was Phyllis, but I could not pronounce it and called her "Fedee," which name clung to her.

When I was about thirteen Mr. Law moved his family to Walthourville, Liberty County, and poor Fleming was forgotten. He forgot "N. J." too and Katie Fleming succeeded me.

A SOUTHERN BELLE

"I was young and happy then."

A new family moved into the village at this time whose plantation was in Liberty County but who had heretofore spent their summers on Wilmington Island near Savannah. They came to Jonesville to have their sons prepared for college by our own teacher. Their names were John, Nathaniel, and Timothy Barnard, "Nat and Tim." Tim and I were the same age. His birthday was the 26th of March, 1834. He was always asking me my age. John soon captured the hearts of all the girls with his gentle courtly manners and pretty brown eyes and hair. If I lost my heart with the others, I kept my secret and would never admit it. Laura admitted to me in after years that she had loved him and that she always knew I did too, although I never said so. Mr. Barnard's elegant plantation house was seven miles from Father's and many a party and dining I attended at their hospitable home.

In the spring of 1847, Father gave Sister an elegant Chickering piano. This added much to our pleasure. She taught me my notes and several pieces and songs. We used to sing duets: "What Are the Wild Waves Saying," "The Evening Breeze," "Hear Me Norma," and others.

The gay season in Liberty County was when the boys returned from college the first of November. For two months, their vacation, we attended dinings and parties, going in our carriages for miles and often returning the same night. When Brother was at home he would escort us, but if not we, Sister and I, would go alone with our faithful coachman Titus, feeling perfectly safe. Sometimes we would spend the night, and during the evening, while we were enjoying ourselves inside, the coachmen would look at us through the windows, enjoying seeing us dance. After the guests were served, they were invited into the kitchen and given a bountiful meal by the hostess. They used to love to take us to the parties and were proud of their "young misses," as they called us. Oh, what happy days those were! What happy evenings we spent!

Our party dress would be of white tarleton, full-flounced skirt, over a large hoop-skirt, with as many as half a dozen stiffly starched white skirts. The larger we stood out, the more stylish we were. Our dresses were low-necked and short-sleeves with white lace berthas and a wide ribbon sash around our waists, pink, blue, or white. It was tied in a big bow and long ends in front or left side. The younger girls wore them tied in the back. Our waists were pointed in front, the skirts gathered full into it all around. The bow was either at the point or turned and tied at the left side. We wore white kid gloves, coming a little above the wrist. Deep white lace was gathered into the edge of the glove, with bracelets worn where the lace began. Sister had some very handsome bracelets. One was garnets set in gold. I used to wear ribbon like my sash tied around the wrist with a bow and streamers about a quarter of a yard long. We wore either a necklace or ribbon to match the sash around our throats, tied in front in a bow and ends. We wore white kid slippers with white rosettes on top and white clocked stockings.

Sister and I used to often wear a natural white camellia in our hair, to one side of knot, and one pinned on our breast. Our hair was worn parted in the middle and drawn down over the ears and puffed out as big as we could get it and held out by little combs made for the purpose. They did not show. We wore earrings, only the lower point of the ear showing. Our hair was oiled and kept perfectly smooth and plastered. Sometimes we wore little "beau-catchers" kept stiff with gum arabic. You can see I went to parties long before I was a young lady through with boarding school.

Sunday, the fifteenth of April, 1849, there was an unusually cold spell of weather. We went to Pleasant Grove Church on the Darien road that morning as there was no service at the Midway Church that day. It began to rain while we were there and to turn cold. We were dressed in light spring dresses and became chilled driving home. That night it turned very cold, and next morning we found everything killed. Corn "waist high" and all the cotton crop killed! Planters had to replant everything, and I have heard Father say he made more that year than usual. This cold spell is remembered now as "the severe cold night in April 1849."

In June of this year Sister, Laura, and I were invited to spend some time on Colonel's Island with our friends Mr. Roswell King and his family. I was then fifteen years of age, and enjoyed my visit so much, I must not fail to tell you of it. Laura, Sister, "Tim" Barnard and I left Jonesville in our carriage and went to Mr. Barnard's plantation. We spent the day there pleasantly, and after dinner we went about a mile to Barnard's Landing on the Riceboro River. Mr. and Mrs. Barnard went with us. We got into his row boat and sat on a buffalo robe in the bottom of the boat. Four of his negro men rowed, singing their boat songs. We had a delightful sail on the river, so new to me, and reached Colonel's Island just as the sun was setting. As we neared the Island we saw Mr. King and family assembled on the shore and waving to us. They received us most cordially.

The family consisted of Mr. and Mrs. King and her dear old mother Mrs. Maxwell, a grown daughter Mary, two grown sons, Audley and Fred, and several other children. My old friend Gus Fleming was there as tutor to the boys. Every day we would go out rowing on the river, crabbing and fishing. We enjoyed many horseback rides. This was a most beautiful and picturesque island. Once I rode horseback with Fred to the Point where the view is grand. We saw the ocean in the distance, and St. Catharine and Ossabaw Islands not far distant. I consider this one of the happiest weeks of my life. We returned to Mr. King's plantation on the mainland in one of his boats, Audley King accompanying us. Their oarsmen sang beautiful boatsongs too as they rowed. Uncle Moses' carriage met us there, and from thence we went back to Jonesville and back to school.

On the thirty-first of December, 1849, Father, Brother, and his negro boy Tom, and I left for Savannah in the carriage before day, arriving there about midday. The next morning Brother and I left for Macon, traveling by the train. This was the first time I had ever ridden on a train, or ever seen one. This road was the Central Railroad, one of the first roads built in Georgia, if not the first. I enjoyed the ride very much, everything being so new to me. As we approached Macon, I saw for the first time hills and red clay roads, having lived in a flat, sandy country near the coast.

[following is missing (page 47) from Midway text; it appears as page 21 and part of page 22 of Martin edition]

We reached Macon after dark, having taken all day to travel 190 miles. We spent the night at Cousin Sarah Weed's, formerly Mrs. William LeConte. The next morning, Brother hired a carriage and we set out for Montpelier Institute, sixteen miles distant in Monroe County. This school for girls was owned and under the supervision of Rt. Rev. Stephen Elliott, first Bishop of Georgia. We were welcomed by Bishop Elliott and invited into his library in Chase Hall, one of the most beautiful of the buildings. Bishop Elliott was an elegant, courtly gentleman of the old school. He greeted me warmly and introduced me to Madam Sophie Sosnowski, one of his teachers. A lady of great culture and refinement, she was a Pole who taught music and German and oil painting. She took me up to her private parlor and introduced me to her daughters, [Midway text resumes] Sophie and Callie, and two other girls, Lizzie Shaw and Matilda Kershaw, who had spent their vacation there.

Bishop Elliott had a beautiful home on a hill opposite the Institute buildings where he and his family resided. Brother dined with him, and Madam Sosnowski took me to the large dining room in Lamar Hall to dinner. There I met the Reverend Seneca G. Bragg, the chaplain. The girls had not yet returned from their vacation in December. The months of May and December were the two vacation months.

Brother returned to Macon that afternoon. I felt sad and lonely. During the day when I had caught glimpses of his red hair, walking about the grounds with the Bishop, my tears flowed freely. For the first time in my life, I knew what homesickness was. I must describe to you this beautiful place. The buildings were situated in spacious grounds with beautiful trees. Around Chase Hall was a lovely flower garden. A large cloth-of-gold rose clambered around the Bishop's study window. Mr. Bragg, a middle-aged bachelor, occupied a pretty little cottage near the chapel. This chapel was a long building with dormitories at one end that was called "the studio." The chapel was a long room, carpeted, with a bench extended along the sides, cushioned. There was a piano and a lectern where the chaplain read prayers every morning for us before breakfast. Miss Wells, from England, one of the music teachers, conducted the music of the service. The service consisted of "Family Morning Prayer," the Psalter for the day, and the Lessons. On Sundays, we had the full morning service at eleven o'clock. One of the girls acted as monitress and sat at the door marking girls who were late or absent from these services, also marked them for absence or tardiness for meals and lessons.

There were two other small one-story buildings of four rooms each. In each room was a piano upon which the girls practiced. Then there was another building consisting of a long room in which Miss Wray from Augusta taught drawing and painting. On the grounds was a large garden in which were two green houses, enclosed in glass, in which were rare potted plants. There were two gardeners; Mr. Carolin attended to the flowers, and the other, a white man too, attended the vegetable garden. The Montpelier Springs were in a ravine between the hill where was the Bishop's residence and the Institute grounds. A long, narrow bridge spanned it. It was a favorite walk of the girls to these springs to get water.

The teachers were all ladies, highly educated, some having been graduated from Miss Willard's school of Troy, New York, a noted school. Miss Martha Buell was the principal, Miss Wells was my music teacher, and I took drawing lessons from Miss Wray. Each teacher had her room and parlor, and the classes recited to her in her own parlor. The girls studied in their rooms, and at the ringing of the bells by the monitress every three quarters of an hour, we went to our classes. Every girl had a schedule of hours tacked up in her room. The bell was in a frame out in the grounds.

The girls occupied dormitories. They were divided into sections under the care of different teachers who went around during the study hours, day and night, seeing if we were studying. At nine o'clock at night, each teacher collected the girls of her section in her parlor and read the "Family Evening Prayer" in the Prayer Book. At ten o'clock, the bell was rung for us to retire. At ten fifteen, each teacher went her rounds to see if every girl was in bed and the lights out. At six o'clock in the morning, the rising bell was rung, prayers at seven, then breakfast about eight o'clock. There were two matrons, Mrs. Atkinson, and her sister, Miss Dodd. Negro servants waited upon the table and made our fires and attended to our rooms. The silver used on the table was solid, the fare plain but good and plentiful. Reverend Mr. Bragg sat at one end of the long table and asked the blessing. If we arrived after the blessing, we were marked. I have often seen the kind old gentleman wait till a hurrying girl reached her seat. I cannot better describe his character than by a tribute paid him by Bishop Elliott, after his death in 1861: "His heart was all love, his tongue all charity; men watched his walk and conversation and believed in Jesus Christ."

During the first week and the next, after I arrived at Montpelier, the students came in from all parts of Georgia, South Carolina, and other states. At this writing, after fifty years, I can remember the names of all the teachers and more than sixty of the students. I think there were about seventy-five altogether while I was there; the tuition $250.00 a year. My most intimate friend was "Jackie" Bates from Covington, Georgia. I have never met her since we parted that fall. I remained at this school one year, studying the highest branches. I was not sick a day, only received one demerit, called "neglect of study hour." My teacher, Miss Lizzie Buell, found me reading a letter from Mother during an hour appointed for study.

January 1st, 1851, Father decided to send me to a college in Madison, Georgia, the Methodist Female College under President Wittich, hoping I would see more of the world by boarding in a private family. Father and I left home about January first and went by steamer from Savannah to Charleston, South Carolina, to meet Brother (Louis), who with our cousin Joseph LeConte was there with Professor Agassiz, on their way to Key West on a scientific expedition. I had the pleasure of being introduced to that distinguished scientist. We spent the day and night at the Charleston Hotel. The next morning, Father and I left for Augusta, Georgia, on the first railroad built in the South. We arrived at night, took supper at the hotel, then took the night train for Madison, where we arrived before day.

Father had a letter of introduction from Judge Nesbit of Macon to Dr. Wingfield. The next morning he and his wife and daughters called. He took Father around and introduced him to the president of the college, then to Dr. Oglesby's, a very nice family of the place where he secured board for me. Father wanted me to enter the senior class, and in order to do so, I had to be examined by the President and Professor Echols, and to my great joy, was told I could enter the senior class. After examining me in several studies, I think their decision was made upon my correctly demonstrating "the 47th proposition of the first book of Mayfair's Euclid." This is considered very difficult. This was the result of Ole Mac's thorough teaching. President Wittich then conducted me to a large schoolroom in the building announcing me at the door, "Mistress Jones, young ladies," leading me to where the senior class was sitting and seating me by Mary Harris of Walton County, afterward the wife of Dr. Chan Jones of Atlanta. Father had remained in Madison that day to hear the result of my examination. You can imagine my delight that I was able to tell him of my success.

I spent a very happy six months in Dr. Oglesby's family and enjoyed going to that school very much. I was graduated in June, would have shared the honors but was told by the president that in consequence of my having been there so short a time he thought it unjust to give it to me. There were eight of us in the graduating class. I read a graduating composition on the subject, "The Power of a Great Name," closing it with the lines, "Lives of great men all remind us we can make our lives sublime," etc. We were all dressed alike in white swiss dresses. They had full tucked skirts, period waists, long sleeves gathered into a cuff of inserting and edging, and a wide band of inserting and edging around the neck. The waist opened at the back, a wide straw colored silk sash, tied around the waist in a big bow and ends a little to the side in front. We wore kid gloves of the same color. Our compositions had blue ribbon on them. My hair was rolled in two pompadour rolls over toward the face on each side, and a French twist in the back. We wore breast pins and earrings.

I stayed at Mrs. Oglesby's two weeks after commencement, waiting for Mr. and Mrs. Barnard who were to take me up to Athens. On Monday morning the fourteenth of July, 1851, I left with them. We went to the hotel, the Newton House, and there, dear children, at the table across from me, at supper, sat the young man who afterwards became my husband, two years exactly from that date! He was pointed out to me by Mr. Barnard as a friend of Brother's. The next day Cousin Josephine Le-Conte, Cousin John's beautiful wife, came over and took me over to her house on the campus. Cousin John was one of the professors in the college. That afternoon as we were walking on the campus, we met this young gentleman coming from the College and going to the Newton House to supper. He was, though only twenty-four years old, a tutor of mathematics in the College. I was introduced to him by Cousin Josephine.

I must describe him to you. He was very fine-looking according to my idea of good looks. He was five feet, nine inches in height, black hair and brown eyes, pretty white teeth and good features. He was dressed in a black frock-tailed coat and white vest. He wore Burnside whiskers—young men did not wear a mustache in those days, nor part their hair in the middle. He was very diffident and a great student, much respected by everyone. A very moral young man, no bad habits, and was a member of the Presbyterian Church. It is unnecessary to give you his name [Thomas Goulding Pond]. He was the grandson of Reverend Thomas Goulding of Liberty County, Georgia, my birthplace. His parents, Dr. Asa and Lucy

Anne Goulding Pond, were living in Columbus, Georgia, having moved there from Lexington, Oglethorpe County, Georgia, where he was born January 31, 1827. His parents and grandparents were eminently pious people and he was brought up as a Christian child should be and was baptized in infancy. He was an intimate friend of Brother's and had been invited by him to be one of his groomsmen at his wedding which was to occur in Athens on the 29th of July.

I had come to Athens to be one of the bridesmaids. Brother was to marry Miss Mary Williams, a very pretty and sweet young lady of that place. All the attendants were invited to take tea at Mrs. Williams's a few nights before the wedding, so that we might get better acquainted. There Mr. Pond and I were thrown together and conversed pleasantly. The wedding, on Thursday night at the home of the bride, was quite a large one, two parlors thrown into one. The bride was a petite brunette, with beautiful black hair and brown eyes, quite a contrast to the groom, who had dark red hair, blue eyes and fair complexion, and was tall.

The bride was dressed in a white silk dress, full skirt, with long lace veil, white orange blossom wreath, white kid gloves and slippers. Brother wore a black swallow-tailed coat, black trousers, a white brocaded silk vest and white silk necktie, white kid gloves. The four bridesmaids wore white tarleton dresses with long pale blue veils and blue gauze ribbon sashes, wreathes of orange flowers and buds, and roses mixed. We wore white kid gloves and slippers. I entered the room first on the arm of Mr. George Hull of Athens. Mr. Pond waited with Miss Mary Frances Williams, a cousin of the bride. Miss Callie Lumpkin, Miss Mary Willis Cobb, and Mr. Robert McCoy and Mr. John Thomas were the others. Rev. Albert Williams, brother of the bride, performed the ceremony. The supper was an elegant one.

The next day, Mr. Hull called for me in a carriage, to call upon the bride and groom. She looked very sweet and modest in an ashes of roses silk "second day" dress. The groom looked very happy and proud of her. It was the custom for the wedding guests to call upon the couple the next day, and refreshments were handed. The next week was very gay, Commencement Week of the college. I attended all the exercises in the day at the chapel and went to parties at night. Mrs. McCoy had given one the week before to Brother and her sister, the bride, where I met Mr. Pond again. I met him too at the other parties and promenaded with him. I went to these parties with Cousin John and Cousin Josephine LeConte. It was not the custom for the young ladies to be escorted by the young gentlemen to them. We were not dependent upon them for escorts. One of these parties was at Chief Justice Lumpkin's, one at Mrs. Ware's, and one at Mrs. Thomas's, and I was invited to one at Dr. Church's, the president of the college, but rain prevented us from going.

Athens was crowded with visitors from all points of Georgia and a great many matches were made there. Several boys from Liberty County were there at college. The Barnards and others were very kind to me. This was my debut into society, and I enjoyed it to the fullest extent.

About a week after commencement, Brother and Sister Mary started off on their bridal trip in upper Georgia, taking me with them. Mr. Pond and Tim and Nat Barnard were at the depot to bid me good-by. I heard afterwards that Sister Mary said to Brother that "Mr. Pond is in love with Nela." We left in the early morning, traveled all day, and reached Atlanta at sunset, and spent the night at Dr. Thompson's, a most un-attractive wooden building where the Kimball House now stands. Atlanta was then a very small village; her name had been changed from Marthasville about two years before. At this writing forty-eight years afterwards, she is a large city of more than 100,000 inhabitants. I remember the small room, lighted by a candle, which I occupied, the wide piazza extending around the front and sides of the house, with the trains coming up to the door.

The next morning we left for Marietta, taking about two hours. We found a pretty town and a very good hotel. We remained there about a week, saw Aunt Robarts and Cousins Mary and Louisa Robarts, her maiden daughters, and took tea with them, meeting our friends Mr. and Mrs. Henry Jones of Liberty County. Our stay in Marietta was very pleasant. From there we went to Cartersville, visiting Sister Mary's sister, Mrs. Andrew Baxter. The country there is beautiful. We visited the Iron Works owned by Hon. Mark A. Cooper. I went to a picnic on horseback on Pine Mountain. Ellen Stovall and Tom Cooper were among the party. Upon my return in company with Mr. Baxter, I rode along the banks of the Etowah River, which is a beautiful stream.

After a stay of about a week, hospitably entertained, we went on to Kingston, Cass County, on the state road. Brother was studying the geology of the country, and one day we joined a party and visited the Saltpeter Cave near that place. I remember well the dark caverns and the stalactites. The guide carried a torch, and we heard there were many bats in the cave. We could hear water flowing and trickling. When we got out in the air again, someone gave us a drink of brandy, it was so cold in the cave.

From Kingston we went to Chattanooga and spent a few days at the hotel. We went in a hack up Lookout Mountain where we spent a week at a boarding house, the only one on the mountain, a plain wooden house kept by a Mr. McCullough. We visited all the points of interest, the Devil's Pulpit and Lookout Point from which we could see three states, and the beautiful Tennessee River at its base. This point is a dangerous place. Returning homeward we stopped at Catoosa Springs for a few days, where there was a large hotel with a piazza all around it. It was quite a resort, but the crowd had all left. Then we came further down to Gordon Springs. We got off at a station and had to ride several miles in the country to the Springs which were kept by Governor Gordon's father. This was a large plain wooden building. The partitions between the rooms only extended to the rafters of the unceiled roof, leaving an open space where one could crawl from one room to another. I was very timid, but Brother was in the adjoining room on one side, but I did not know who was in the room on the other side. You can see what a plain unfinished building it was.

The season was about over. There were a few people still there. One day while we were there, Mr. John B. Gordon, afterward a Governor of Georgia, got up a picnic at Silver Springs, fifteen miles distant. A party of young ladies and gentlemen, I among them, went on horseback, and in a buggy. The country through which we rode was wild-looking, high hills, and deep ravines. The Spring was fifteen feet deep, the water so clear that you could drop a pebble in it and see it at the bottom. We enjoyed the day very much, and did not arrive at the Gordon Springs until eleven o'clock that night. As we travelled through that wild country, the road winding along the edge of a high precipice at one place, I was alarmed. I came back in the buggy with Mr. Gordon as it was dangerous to ride horseback in the dark. I found Sister Mary had been very uneasy about me, and she and Brother were much relieved when I returned in safety. An old lady was heard complaining at "the noise those thoughtless young people had made, returning so late and disturbing people's rest." Those fashionable Springs are never heard of now though they were very popular fifty years ago.

The wedding tour was now drawing to a close. On our way back to Athens, we spent the night at Stone Mountain, and to this day I can remember the appetite with which I enjoyed the fried ham and eggs and good biscuits that we had for supper there. The next afternoon we arrived in Athens after a most delightful month spent in the mountains of upper Georgia.

I was invited to spend the month of October with Mrs. Williams, where Brother and Sister Mary lived. It was this month on the night of the 11th of October, that I promised your father to be his wife. We reached Athens about the 19th of September, so you see that even then he showed his disposition to be "always in a hurry." He always regretted in after years that he had not obtained my father's permission to address me before doing so. The first flower he gave me was a tube rose, and to the day of his death, whenever he could, he would bring one to me. We always called it "our flower." The first book he presented me with was "David Copperfield," by Charles Dickens; it had just come out. I was then seventeen, and he was twenty-four, both strong and full of life and hope.

The last of October, I returned to Liberty County. Brother went as far as Macon with me, where a fair was in progress. We went by Atlanta and travelled all day and night. He put me in care of Nat and Tim Barnard, and we took the Central train to Savannah. I spent the night at Cousin Sam Cassels', who was

Principal of Chatham Academy. The next day we took the stage to Riceboro, where Father met me with his carriage. I had been absent ten months from home. The family was still at our summer home in Jonesville, and I was delighted to see them all again. They were in the midst of preparation for moving back to the plantation, and the next day we went. I had developed very much, and Laura remarked that I looked "quite like a young lady."

I did not keep my engagement secret long, but soon told Mother and Sister. As Mr. Pond was a grandson of Dr. Goulding, formerly of Liberty County, they were much pleased. He had vacation during November and December. He went home to Columbus first to visit his parents, then came down to Liberty County to see me. He came out from Savannah in the stage coach with one of his college mates from Liberty. He saw a gentleman sitting in his buggy with two iron-gray horses at the wharf. Upon inquiry as to who it was, his companion told him it was "Mr. William Jones." He went into Riceboro, took a room and commenced to shave. While his face was white with lather, there was a knock at the door. When he called, "Come in," who should come in but "Mr. William Jones." He introduced himself and invited him to go home with him in the buggy. This invitation Mr. Pond gladly accepted.

I was dressed, waiting upstairs in my room and watched them as they drove through the big gate up the avenue to the house. I took good care though that they did not see me. Sister's maid Liza, not hiding behind the curtains like Sister and I, took a good look and exclaimed, "Oh, Miss Nela, what a han'some young man Mr. Pond is!" I saw him as he jumped out of the buggy looking so nice, dressed in a black Prince Albert suit, with black grosgrain silk vest and black silk hat. I was so modest that I would not go downstairs until Father sent Fedee, the housemaid, for me. I felt very much confused and shy. When I entered they were talking and examining some little Chinese idols on the mantel that Cousin Richard Way had sent from China, where he was living as a missionary. I had to summon all my courage to go in and meet him before Father, but he soon left us to ourselves. I introduced him to the rest of the family with pride.

The next day Mother invited him to spend the rest of his visit with us, saying if he would, she would send to Riceboro for his trunk. This invitation he was delighted to accept. The time passed so happily that I remember very little about it. We used to take drives along the quiet country roads and often sat out on the lawn in the sunshine and eat sugarcane which he delighted to peel and cut for me. Father had a plenty of it. We sometimes visited the syrup mill and watched them grind the cane and make syrup. All the negroes were looking at him, admiring him as I thought. When Titus would bring the buggy around for us to go to drive, Mr. Pond would "tip" him and his mother, old Mum Chloe said, "Mr. Pond gave Ti his start in de wull." We took him to Midway Church the next Sunday, and there he was introduced to many of my relatives and friends. During this visit he asked Father's permission to correspond with me, which was granted.

He returned to Columbus after staying with us about a week, and in the latter part of December, he came back again and made me another visit. It was then he brought me a gold medallion containing his daguerreotype which he had had taken in Savannah for me. I have it still, have had it for forty-eight years. It was considered a good likeness, and I hope it will be taken care of and always kept in the family, greatly treasured. He returned to Athens January 1st and resumed his duties as tutor of mathematics in the College. This was the beginning of 1852. I spent this year very quietly at home corresponding with him about twice a week. Father would hand me my letters, and I would often read portions to Mother, omitting the love passages.

In April, Mr. Vandenberg, a music teacher living in Savannah, began coming out once a week to Liberty to give lessons in the county. He would spend a night at Father's every week giving us each two lessons, one at night and one in the morning. I took my morning lesson before breakfast. If I was late, he would go to the piano and bang to call me down. He was a splendid teacher. He would come in his buggy. There was no railroad in those days south of Savannah. Sister and I practiced hard. We practiced about three hours a day apiece, till Mother was tired out with the noise.

In May we moved to Jonesville and carried the piano with us. The most important event in this year was the advent of the first grandchild in the family, born to Brother and Sister Mary in Athens, Georgia, little William Jones, June 5th, 1852. We were very proud of him. In August, Father, Mother, and Sam, fourteen years old, went up to Athens to attend Commencement and to see the new baby. Poor Sam's first trip up the country was spoiled by his taking mumps, and he had to stay home at Brother's missing everything. Nobody knew where he got it. After Commencement, during a short vacation, Mr. Pond had intended visiting me but was prevented by the illness of his brother Henry, who was at College. But he came down in November, and again in December, that time staying two weeks.

On the November visit, he came out in a hired conveyance, which he kept during his stay of a few days paying four dollars a day for it. In December, when he came, I would not allow this, being always economical, and so he was enabled to make a long visit, two weeks. In November, Brother brought his wife and little baby down to visit his old home. Little Willie was a lovely baby, the first one in our family for fourteen years and much beloved by us.

On the 5th, 6th, and 7th of December, there was a centennial of the settlement of the county in 1752. We attended all the exercises at Midway Church, heard the sermons by Rev. I.S.K. Axson on Sunday, the address by Mr. John B. Mallard on Monday when the cornerstone was laid for a monument to be erected in honor of the first settlers of the county. Judge William Law, of Savannah, a native of Liberty County, delivered a most beautiful address on Tuesday. The monument was to have been erected in front of the Church. Tables were spread bountifully with delightful refreshments nearby. Toasts were given, and it was a delightful reunion of the county. The Chatham Artillery came from Savannah by invitation with a German brass band which furnished inspiring music. The Artillery's cannon boomed each morning to announce the beginning of the festivities of the day.

I was young and happy then, and enjoyed it to the full, laughing and talking with my young friends of both sexes. I was then in my nineteenth year. This was an [un]usually gay month. I attended several parties, one very pleasant one at the home of Mr. John Barnard, to which nearly all the young people of the county were invited. New Year, 1853, opened with the sudden death of my own dear young friend, Tim Barnard. He was only ill a few days with erysipelas and died on the

5th of January. Just two weeks before, I had danced with him in those parlors, full of life and hope. This produced a great impression upon me, "one shall be taken and the other left." This put an end to all gaieties and saddened the whole community. Mr. Pond attended the funeral with us. He and all the college boys left soon after for Athens.

HOMEMAKING IN
THE OLD SOUTH

"Nothing special to do, surrounded by plenty."

n February, 1853, he [Thomas Goulding Pond] resigned his position in the College and accepted the
professorship of mathematics in the Tuskegee Female College. Our friend, Mr. Henry Holcombe Bacon of Liberty County, was the president. Before
leaving for his new home, he came down to Liberty
to make me a visit and 'twas then that we appointed
the 14th of July as our wedding day. The members
of the sophomore class of 1853 of Franklin College
presented him, when he left Athens, an elegant fob
chain with a large seal attached to it. The stone was
a beautiful cornelian. It is still in my possession to
be given to his son Thomas Asa. Only the preceding
year, one of the classes presented him with a handsome gold-headed cane. This was subsequently lost
when our house burned in Savannah in 1857.

In the Spring of 1853, Sister and Father and I went in our carriage to Savannah to buy my trousseau. My generous father did not limit us but told us to get just what we wanted. We went to Mrs. Branch, from whom Father had always gotten our bonnets, consulted with her as to what I would need of everything. We bought from her a long white tulle veil bordered with lace and a wreath of orange blossoms, a white crepe bonnet trimmed with delicate white and lilac flowers on the outside, and delicate pink and white flowers in a ruche in the inside. It had white gauze ribbon to be tied in a large bow under the chin. This bonnet was a "cottage shape." A white crepe cape at the back concealed the back of my neck. Where it joined the bonnet was a tiny delicate wreath of white flowers, tiny roses. This was a beautiful bonnet. It cost $11.00, a high price for a summer bonnet. My travelling bonnet was of white straw, the same shape, trimmed with wide apple green silk ribbon with cape made of the ribbon, wide bow under the chin. The green was becoming to me, as I had color and auburn hair. The inside of the bonnet was lined with shirred corn-colored silk. No flowers on my travelling bonnet, of course. My bridal gown was of white crepe de Paris, a fabric much used then resembling a summer silk, only a thinner material. I got this at Mr. Nevitt's dry goods store, *the* store of Savannah in those days. I bought a handsome wide white brocade silk sash, a handsome white lace bertha, white kid gloves. White silk boots tipped with white kid completed the bridal attire.

My "second day dress" was solid colored "ashes of roses" silk. I also bought a lovely light blue crepe de Paris dress, a beautiful berege, light gray ground with bouquets of pink flowers on it. This dress was trimmed on waist and sleeves with pink gauze ribbons. My ashes of roses dress was trimmed with lilac ribbons. I bought a white dotted swiss, trimmed with edging, a plain white swiss trimmed with edging and inserting, a plain white nansook trimmed with embroidery, which I wore to breakfast the next morning after the wedding with little bronze slippers with blue rosettes, a lemon colored cambric and muslins and ginghams. I bought a dark blue chambray travelling dress, trimmed with wavy white and blue braids; a mantilla of the same goods was worn with it. In those days no lady ever appeared in public without a covering. In summer they were made of silk or lace with silk appliqued upon it, pinned low on the shoulders, with gold pins, for the purpose. I had an elegant white silk one, and one of the same material as my ashes of roses silk, a black silk one with pinked edges for ordinary wear with any kind of dress, calico or lawn, etc.

My bridal dress and my silk were made in Savannah by a fashionable mantua-maker, Mrs. Hasselt. My bridal dress was a full skirt flounced up to the waist. Each flounce was from six to eight inches at the waist and growing deeper towards the bottom of the skirt. Every flounce was edged with narrow white satin ribbon. The waist was made low-necked and short sleeves. The bertha nearly hid the waist. I wore a bouquet of white artificial flowers to match the wreath, on my breast. The veil falling to the edge of my skirt behind enveloped me except for my face. The orange wreath was flat on the head in front, coming to a point in front, with little buds, and falling behind each ear on the neck in full bunches of orange flowers and roses. The hair was worn puffed over the ears. I wore long gold earrings with breast pin to match.

While I was in Savannah, I had a daguerreotype taken of myself which I sent to Mr. Pond. I also bought him an elegant gold ring with a cornelian stone in it. Mother had our seamstress, Nellie, make me as many articles of underthings as I needed, all by hand. The other dresses were made at home too by this faithful servant, superintended by Mother and Sister. I must say I did very little on my trousseau. Father and Mother made preparations for a large wedding. They ordered fruit and plain pound cakes made at a Savannah bakery, West India fruit and candies. We issued invitations to about fifty people. As our Jonesville house was not large enough to hold all our friends, we had to limit our guests to our nearest relatives and friends. We were related to nearly every family in the county.

On Saturday evening, July 9th, Mr. Pond arrived with his sister, Callie, in a buggy which he hired in Savannah. She was a lovely young lady and won all our hearts at once by her sweet, affectionate manner. The following Monday, Mr. Pond and I took an early morning ride, and he left for Savannah to remain there until Thursday, the 14th, as there was no hotel in the county to entertain him. We all went to the village church on Sunday, and I felt very diffident. This was a very busy week. Dear Mother and Sister were so interested in the cake baking and decorating the house, etc. Friends from all parts of the county came pouring into the village.

On Thursday morning, a lovely day, our friends came over to arrange the table. Cousin Ann Stevens had our carpenter make a little "temple of love," as she said, of wood. She covered it entirely with flowers and evergreens. That night she put in it a lighted candle. This made a pretty ornament for the center of the long table put diagonally across the room. Before dark, old Aunt Shearer, Father's aunt, came in her little carriage drawn by her maid. This was the same little buggy that her sister, my grandmother Jones, used to use before she died. She was about seventy-three and a dear interesting old lady much loved by us all, and I was much complimented at her coming.

Soon after the house was lighted up, the guests began to assemble. Sister came running upstairs to tell me that the groom had arrived with one of his groomsmen. They had come in a carriage from Savannah—forty miles. The stage had come that same day, but he wanted a carriage at his disposal. He had gone to an inn in Riceboro and dressed, then driven the seven miles to Jonesville, arriving after dark. I asked Sister how he looked. She replied, "just as handsome as can be." He was dressed in a black evening suit, swallow-tail coat, white vest, white silk necktie, and white kid gloves. Sister and her maid Liza dressed me. The bridesmaids were my cousins, Annie Quarterman and Matilda Harden, Sister, and Mr. Pond's sister, Callie. They were dressed in white tulle over white silk, white wreathes, white sashes, white gloves and slippers. The groomsmen were dressed like the groom. Mr. Henry Law of Savannah waited with Sister, Mr. Robert Mallard of Liberty County with Callie, Mr. Hugh King of Alabama with Annie Quarterman and Sam with Matilda Harden. The groom and his groomsmen were invited upstairs where they paired off with the bridesmaids in the hall and went downstairs.

I told Liza that when the last couple left to go down to open the door for me. She did so, and I came out, trembling and excited, took the groom's arm and went down into the parlor. Two couples stood on each side leaving a space for us to stand. Reverend Dr. Axson, my beloved pastor, officiated. I can remember now where Father and Mother stood and watched us, though I stood with bowed head and tremblingly bowed assent, but the groom said distinctly, "I will." We were not married with the ring, which I regret, but he gave me one with the inscription in it, "T.G.P. to M.C.J., 14 July, 1853," which I now have. I wore it till my hand was so disfigured with rheumatism that I could not wear it any longer. But I still have it, and I hope you children will always keep it sacredly.

After the ceremony, congratulations followed. Then soon, two servants entered, one carrying a waiter with plain and fruit cake iced and little plates and napkins, and the other with a waiter bearing glasses of iced lemonade. I was sitting by the groom when his first groomsman, Mr. Henry Law, stepped up to us calling me by my new name, "Mrs. Pond," asked me what I would take. The name startled and thrilled me, and for the first time I realized the great step I had taken. It was the custom for the groomsmen to go around with the waiter and help the ladies. I become excited now as I recall it all more than forty-six years ago.

About eleven o'clock supper was announced. Mr. Pond and I led the way to the dining room and took our place at the head of the table. All the guests stood around the table. The supper was most bountiful and elegant. I can remember that there was cold sliced turkey, ham and smoked tongue, loaf bread, nice biscuits, pickles, jellies, pound cakes, fruit cakes, ice cream, gelatin, and syllabub, candies, and tropical fruits. I remember eating only some ice cream and cake. The gentlemen conducted the ladies back to the parlor after they had eaten, then they returned to the dining room and ate, as was the custom in those days.

There was a Chinaman at my wedding. He had been brought over from China as a nurse by Cousin Susan Way, whose husband, Cousin Richard Way, had been a missionary in China. His name was "Asoom." He had a curiosity to see an American wedding and supper. He was dressed in Chinese costume and was interested in everything. Father took pleasure in showing him the bride and the table. Poor Callie had a terrible sick headache all day, could scarcely dress, but the excitement cured her completely. She was among the gayest of the girls that night.

It had not become then the custom to give wedding presents, as it has since, but my dear friend, Mrs. Barnard, gave me a very pretty silver card case, which I gave to my daughter Anne on her wedding day. A silver butter knife from Annie Quarterman, a silver pocket-fruit knife from Corinne Quarterman, a silver pickle knife and fork from Matilda Harden, a pair of vases from Callie, a pair of toilet bottles from Sister. Father gave us $150.00.

The next day we invited the bridal party and other friends to accompany us to the plantation to a picnic. We spent a pleasant day, spread a table in the large hall where it was cool. We enjoyed plenty of watermelons and lots of other good things. The next day I received my calls. Dr. Axson startled me by asking me, "Where is your lord this morning?" Sunday we went to church, where I wore my beautiful white bonnet and the blue crepe de Paris with white silk mantilla and straw colored gloves. All my dresses that summer were cut low in front to be worn with chemisettes. We stayed at Father's three weeks, when we left by stage to Savannah, thence to Columbus. After telling everybody good-by at Jonesville, all the servants too, we went on to the plantation to bid Father good-by, and many of the negroes came up to the carriage to tell me good-by too. When Father told Mr. Pond to take good care of me and to remember he had given him one of his little chickens, I broke down completely. Callie and I cried all the way to Riceboro. Sam and Mr. Pond laughed and talked, trying to cheer us up.

At Riceboro, we took the stage for Savannah, arriving there about sunset. We took supper at the Pulaski House, then took the Central train for Columbus. We arrived there about one o'clock next day and were met cordially by Mr. Pond's father, Dr. Pond, at the depot. We went up to the home in an omnibus. The family ran out to the gate to meet us. Your grandmother threw her arms around my neck, saying "Welcome, my daughter!" Your Aunt Annie brought your cousin, Ellen Hungerford, a little girl of three years, to meet us in her arms. She is now a grandmother. Your Uncle Will, a pretty little boy of six years, ran out in front of the horses, and frightened us. Your Uncle Henry, a handsome man of nineteen years, and Uncle George, a boy of fourteen on crutches (having hurt his foot on a stone the fall before), were also there. Your Aunt Mag was a little girl of eleven years. She admired my trousseau so much. Your Aunt Cornelia Hungerford came over after dinner, bringing her little six month old, Lucy Goulding. Aunt Cornelia (Pussie) is now a great-grandmother. The servants all came out to meet us. Phyllis and old Aunt Flora I remember particularly — glad to shake hands with their young master's bride. Mrs. Pond took me into a lovely room which she had prepared for us. I had brought them one of my large, two pound wedding fruit cakes beautifully iced and trimmed with gold leaf. The next [day] your grandmother gave a large family dining, and this cake was put in the center of the table. We spent three weeks very delightfully there, and their kindness and love I have never forgotten. Their friends called upon me. While there, your Aunt Cornelia gave us a tea, inviting all the family and some friends, which was much enjoyed.

About September 1st, we left for Tuskegee, Alabama, taking

the stage to Opelika, Alabama, there being no railroad there then. We took the train the rest of the way, arriving about sunset. We boarded in a private family, Mr. and Mrs. Charles Reid, very pleasant people. Their kindness to us I shall never forget, her sympathy for me, so young and a stranger. I formed a strong attachment for both of them. All the prominent people called upon us. I was receiving calls for several weeks. One day your father took me over to the College to return Mrs. Bacon's call. There I was confronted by seventy-five girls out on the lawn and piazzas anxious to see the bride of their professor of mathematics. Mr. and Mrs. Bacon were so cordial, and I was so glad to meet anyone from Liberty County. They only had one little daughter, two years old, Georgia. Your father and I returned many calls together. We used to go to church every Sunday and were invited to sit with the choir, which was downstairs. There were two other brides in the choir, and we three used to sit side by side. I had very little to do, spent my time reading principally. When the schoolgirls would come home from school, those who boarded with Mrs. Reid, I used to go out doors and frolic with them.

Your father was a great reader and never wasted any time, always improving his mind. Every evening he pored over his books and papers till late. Our only light was from wax candles. I used to be lonely during school hours. We spent four happy months in this pleasant family. At Christmas they sold their house, so we went in the New Year to board at the College. We had a large room right across from your father's recitation room on the second floor. About a week before Christmas, Mr. Pond sent me in a closed livery stable carriage with Mr. Reid's nephew, Reid Smith, a boy about fifteen, through the country to Columbus. Your father rode horseback with us for several miles on our journey. He joined me in a week, and we spent the Christmas holidays very happily with his family.

I wanted to buy winter clothes but was ashamed to ask him for the money, so Callie kindly managed it for me. I remember buying a new bonnet and other things. Children, you remember how generous your father always was. He liked to give me everything I wanted, but his mind was always on his books, and he did not know I needed the clothes. One day while walking in the garden that fall in Tuskegee, he noticed my miserable look and made me tell him the trouble. With great effort I told him I wanted $10.00. You ought to have seen his pleasure and alacrity in giving it to me. Yet in Columbus I was still ashamed to ask him.

While in Columbus, Father sent me my little maid Kate. I was so glad to see her. In her trunk I found eight new shirts that Mother had had Nellie, the seamstress, make for your father. Also, "Baxter's Call to the Unconverted" for me. Mother had Kate's trunk key tied on a tape around her neck under her dress. James LeConte brought her as far as Macon, then put her in the care of the conductor to Columbus. She was about twelve years old. Father had given her to me as a deed of gift about two years before. She was a good and faithful servant and remained with me until after freedom. We took her back to Tuskegee January 1st, by the same route of the previous summer, and she waited upon me and attended to my room at the College. Not having much to do, I taught her to read and spell. When I returned, I found that one of the brides had died, Mrs. Root.

We passed a pleasant winter, at the College, with Mr. and Mrs. Bacon and the teachers. After the Commencement, in

June, Mr. Pond resigned his professorship, not thinking his salary sufficient. We spent about a week in Columbus, then went down to Liberty County where I was very happy to be again in the bosom of my family. So glad to see the old home, the servants, and everything and everybody.

That fall your father was elected Professor of Mathematics in the Chatham Academy of Savannah. Owing to yellow fever being in the city that summer, 1854, the school did not open till November. He went down to get ready for me and secured board at a nice house on Barnard St. kept by Mrs. Nevitt. I followed about the middle of November, carrying Kate with me. We spent the Christmas holidays at the dear old plantation which I loved so dearly.

I forgot to tell you that when I was about twelve, Father had added to his house, making the addition of four large rooms, two above and two below with a wide hall between in front of the old house. There was a porch in front reaching to the roof of the house with four large square brick pillars plastered white. The house was painted white with green blinds. The banisters were wide of solid brick plastered and cemented with gray cement. Broad steps with brick balustrades up the sides. He had enlarged his flower garden and had many rare flowers growing. Christmas on the plantation was a great holiday for the negroes. They used to come up to the house on Christmas morning and wish us Merry Christmas, always looking for gifts.

We returned to Savannah about the first of the year (1855) and rented a house in a brick tenement building on St. Julian St. near Christ Church. We used to go there Sunday nights. Father, Mother, and Sister took great interest in our going to house-keeping, and on January 8th, Father came to Savannah in the stage to furnish our house for us. He sent a wagon from the plantation loaded with bedding and bed-clothing, house-hold linen, hams and country produce, and more things than I can remember. In the wagon was Kate's mother, Belle, who was to be our cook, and Sister's maid, Eliza. The next morning I went to our new home, and Father went downtown and sent up furniture: parlors, dining-room, bedrooms, and kitchen. Also groceries—what a dear, good father I had! He spent the first night with us in our new home. I felt like a little girl with her doll house, so proud of my new crockery and furniture. Father went to market the first day and bought our dinner for us. He enjoyed helping us. The next morning your father was out early and bought us oysters and baker's bread etc. for breakfast. I was busy for days getting my house to rights. Father left in a few days, when Sister came down and spent the winter with us. We spent our time delightfully, walking, and shopping, and visiting.

The principal of the Academy was Mr. William Bogart, a Churchman, and became a warm friend of your father, which friendship lasted all their lives. In the Spring, this was 1855 now, Mother and Father made us a visit, and in June, Sister and I took two young lady friends, Cornelia Linet and Mary Alcott, out to Liberty to spend two weeks with us at the plantation. They were charmed with our home, and we enjoyed driving along the country roads, and took walks, picking wild flowers. August and September, Mr. Pond and I went to Jonesville to spend his vacation. Father gave Mr. Pond the use of a horse, Tom, to ride wherever he wanted to. He would gather wild flowers, and bring them home to show Father. He commenced the study of Botany under Father, which gave him pleasure all his life. I often think of those days, when I had nothing special to do, surrounded by plenty.

The first of October, we returned to Savannah and rented another house on a more fashionable street, corner of Liberty and Abercorn, opposite to the home of the Sisters of Mercy. Your father rented a pew in St. John's Church this year. We had been attending the Independent Church, Presbyterian, before this. From association with Mr. Bogart, he was becoming interested in the Episcopal church, reading books on that subject. Just before Christmas Callie and his grandmother, Mrs. Anne Goulding, made us a visit. She was a very handsome old lady about sixty-nine years old, very active and entertaining. She made us some very nice mincemeat like it was made in New England, her birthplace. She made us a present at that time of a set of six solid teaspoons and a set of silver castors. After a visit of two weeks to us, she left for Darien, Georgia, to visit her son, the Reverend Francis R. Goulding, pastor of the Presbyterian Church there and author of "The Young Marooners" and other books. Callie spent the winter with us.

The first of the year, George came down and spent two months or so with us and took private lessons from your father. Sister and Father and Mother made us a visit in March and took Callie back with them to spend a month. George returned to Columbus and we were left alone. Your father was a great reader, and the evenings were very dull for me. I was often homesick for the old plantation home. I would think of Mother and Father sitting one on each side of the fireplace, and Sister there. Sam was passing his last year at Franklin College at Athens (1856).

But my days of idleness and loneliness were now drawing to

a close. On the night of the thirteenth of April, Sunday night, at fifteen minutes to nine o'clock, our home was brightened by the advent of a dear little daughter. Never were young parents happier. Her first cry was music to our ears. Mr. Pond wrote the joyful news to my mother, and she and Callie came in the stage on Tuesday evening. All were so proud of and anxious to see the new baby. Mother brought Nellie to wait on me and also good things from the country, and also brought a little maid named Fannie to leave with me, thinking I would need more help now. This was the second little granddaughter in the family. Brother's little daughter, Rosa, had come November, 1853.

In about two weeks, Father and Sister came down full of curiosity to see my baby. Of course, we thought she was beautiful, and when she got old enough for me to send on the streets, I was proud of her and would ask Kate what people said about her. We could not find any name that we thought pretty enough for her. When she was three months old the pupils of Chatham Academy presented her with a silver knife, fork, and spoon in a case. They wanted to have her initials engraved on them, but we had not yet decided on a name. We finally decided to call her Lucy Tallulah, Lucy for her grandmother Pond.

Callie returned to Columbus in May, and the following vacation we spent in Jonesville. The servants all ran out to the carriage to see Miss Nela's baby. This was the last trip I took to Liberty by the stage, as the S. F. & W. Railroad was then being built. The following Christmas when I went home, I travelled on the cars part of the way.

Nothing occurred particularly this year. All my time was given up to my baby. The following summer we spent our vacation in Columbus to show our baby to her other grandparents and aunts and uncles. We took Belle to mind her, sending Kate and Fannie out to the country. On the 9th of August this year (1856), our dear little nephew Willie died of diphtheria near Madison, Georgia. This cast a gloom over our family. He was five years old and so bright and pretty.

While we were in Columbus, we all celebrated Grandmother Pond's fiftieth birthday by baking a large cake, icing it, and putting the number "50" on top of it. We all went over to Grandmother Goulding's, who lived next door, and took the cake on a silver waiter, where we cut and ate it, little Lucy Tallulah and little Georgia Hungerford bringing up the rear, in their nurses' arms. We enjoyed this vacation very much. In September we went to Madison and spent about ten days with Brother, who was living on his plantation near there. I was anxious for them to see my baby. We found them very sad, but they made us have a pleasant time. I met many of the friends of my college days here. We left for home the last week of September and spent the night in Augusta.

Early the next morning when we were on the train, your father bought the morning paper and told me not to take it too much to heart, but that our house in Savannah had been burnt down the night before, and everything was lost. He carried an insurance of $700.00 on the furniture. The house was a rented one, but it grieved us very much, as we lost things that could not be replaced. Our valuable library was lost, books that we had collected during our youth and the many presents given us by our parents and friends. All we had now was what was in our trunks. We spent the night and day at the Pulaski House, and I went downtown and bought what we needed, then went out to my haven, the old Liberty County home, Jonesville. Then followed the severe illness of our dear little baby, then eighteen months old. For two weeks she lingered between life and death with cholera infantum, but God mercifully spared her to us. Your father was with me during her illness. He returned to Savannah and rented a nice brick house, corner of Tattnall and Wayne Streets, and bought new furniture and had it ready for me when I rejoined him in November.

Before I go further I must describe this summer home of Father's in Jonesville. It was a two-story house with a wide piazza extending across the front and on each side, six rooms downstairs and two above with hall upstairs and down. The house was painted white with green shutters. The beauty of this place was the trees. In the yard were four large red oak trees and five beautiful Lombardy poplars in a row by the palings. The yard was full of lagerstroemia, or crepe myrtle, full of pink and red bunches of flowers during the summer. Cypress vines and morning glories climbed on trellises. We had lots of old maids and lady slippers, but we did not have as lovely a garden there as at the plantation. Lightning struck one of these large oaks one Sunday while we were sitting in the parlor near it, and frightened us very much and killed the tree. The severe hurricane on the 8th of September, 1854, blew down two others of the large oaks, and the hurricane of 1858 blew down the last one—the fourth, and the poplars died. So Father and Mother set out new trees which were growing beautifully when I left the county the last time. Your father and I were both in Jonesville during both of those hurricanes, and they were the severest storms we had ever witnessed. They blew down many of the beautiful oaks that ornamented the village, but no lives were lost and no houses were blown down.

Sister returned to Savannah with me that fall, and we found

that your father had furnished the house beautifully and had tried in every way to keep me from missing the things we had lost in the fire. The furniture was, if anything, handsomer than that we had before. This was a nice brick house with water and gas and bathroom. My father sent us a nice cow from the country, named Mollie, and we were very comfortable and happy and began again to collect the library.

Our little daughter was beginning to talk. One day when I was out walking, she began to fret for me, so her nurse, Mum Belle, took her up to my room saying, "less go look for your maa." When she opened the door, the baby looked all around and surprised Mum Belle by saying, "No Maa here." She developed very rapidly, and during that winter before she was two years old, I had taught her several of Mother Goose's verses. I remember she surprised Mr. Bogart by saying "Itty Bo Peep 'E Yawt 'e teep, an dunno way fine 'em. Yemm yone, tum home, Bing tay ahine 'em." She knew "Little Boy Blue," "Pussy-cat, pussy-cat, where have you been," and "Little Willie Winky" in her baby language. It was so interesting to us to see her little mind develop. She had little short curls all over her head and was so fat and rosy.

On the 20th of February, 1858, we were again made happy by the birth of "another sweet little daughter," as your father always called the little girls as they came. This was little Mary Cornelia. She had auburn hair, blue eyes and fair complexion, was very petite. Mother, Father, Sister, and Nellie came down to see our second little baby. We had every comfort. Your father received a good salary, $1400.00, and we had three servants. I often think of those days. Nellie had made my baby a complete set of infant's clothing. I had very little to do. Father used to

give me from $500 to $600 a year, and you see we wanted
for nothing, though I was always economical. In March, your
grandmother Pond and little eleven years-old Willie came and
made us a visit of a month. They came on the 20th of March;
my baby was four weeks old, and I was perfectly well. While
they were there our grandmother Goulding came too. They
enjoyed so much the oysters, fish, and West India fruit we had
for them. We entertained our relatives from the country, and
all members of the family passing through the city. Your father
used to take Fannie, bearing a big basket, to the market and
she would bring back many nice things. We enjoyed the fine
shad and sausages, celery, oysters, baker's bread, etc.

It was during your grandmother Pond's visit that Edward
Everett came to Savannah, delivering the "Mt. Vernon Lec-
tures." The money was devoted to a fund to help the "Ladies
Mt. Vernon Association" buy the property. Your father took
your grandmother and me to hear him lecture. The following
summer we spent the vacation in Jonesville, and the next winter, about the first of 1859, my aunt, Mrs. Renchie Burton,
came from LaFayette, Alabama, where she had moved, to see
her relatives in Liberty; then she came to Savannah to visit us.
She brought her daughter Augusta, a girl of sixteen. This was
the only time I remember seeing my aunt. We enjoyed her
visit very much and showed her all the respect and affection
we could. During her visit we had the little ambrotype of little
Lucy taken, which she now has. My old pastor, Dr. Axson, had
been called to the Independent Church of Savannah, and in
March 1859, I connected myself with the Presbyterian Church,
and your father took a pew in that church.

The following summer we spent our vacation in Columbus,
taking our two sweet little daughters and Belle, their nurse.

Never were parents prouder of little girls than we were. They had rosy cheeks and curly hair. On October 13th of the year 1859, Sam, who had taken two courses of medicine in Charleston, South Carolina, and was now a practitioner, went to Athens and married Miss Mary Baxter Hayes. The ceremony was performed in the Methodist Church by Dr. Eustace Speer. He had become engaged to her while a student at College. In November, he brought his bride to Savannah to visit us on his way to Liberty. They arrived before breakfast. Your father met them at the depot. Never shall I forget how lovely she was in appearance and manners. We welcomed her as a sister and always loved her as such. They were a handsome couple. He was twenty-one years and she was a few months younger. She had a handsome trousseau, and we had many pleasant walks together through the city. They spent the winter at my father's home. Father bought during that year and fitted up a beautiful home for them at Cedar Hill, a plantation about three miles from his, where they lived during the winters until after the War.

Your Aunt Annie Pond came down to Savannah and spent the winter of 1859 and 1860, arriving the day before Christmas. She was a very pretty young lady, a brunette, black hair and eyes, and a sweet disposition. She petted my children very much. Grandmother Goulding joined her in the spring, returning from her usual visit to Darien. The first of June, Sam and Mary came to see us on their way to Athens, where they spent the summer. I had promised Mary some sherbet when she came, and I had it ready for them. The weather was very hot, and Mary enjoyed it very much. On the 30th of July, their little daughter, Maggie Alethea, was born. We always called her Lila, but her grandmother called her Lily. She was a lovely baby and has always been a great favorite in the family. We went to Jonesville the last of July, and Sunday, the 26th of August, at six o'clock p.m., we were blessed with "another sweet little daughter," Alice Goulding. She was a very fine large baby. I returned to Savannah the last of October.

A DAUGHTER
OF THE CONFEDERACY

"Imagine our despair."

t was that fall that Abraham Lincoln, Republican, was elected president of the United States. There were three Democrat candidates: Bell, Breckenridge, and Douglas. I remember well the excitement in the South. I often heard the conversations between your grandfather and father about politics. Once when I asked Father what would be the result if Lincoln were elected, he replied "War." I never shall forget with what horror that answer filled me. The thought of giving up my young husband and home was more than I thought I could bear. In December, South Carolina, the smallest of the Southern States, seceded from the United States, and Georgia followed her example in January of 1861. Savannah was delighted. I recall a torchlight pro-

59

cession. Men carried lighted transparencies with pictures of Abe Lincoln on them. The other states fell into line and soon Montgomery, Alabama, was made the capital of the Confederate States with Jefferson Davis, President, and Alexander Stephens Vice-president.

Your father having decided to leave the Presbyterian Church, I thought it best to go with him by Dr. Axson's advice, so he rented a pew in St. John's Church again, and on the 31st of March, Easter night, we were confirmed, kneeling by each other's side in that church, by Rt. Rev. Stephen Elliott, D.D., Bishop of Georgia, being presented by the Rev. George H. Clark, the rector. The church was crowded, the service beautiful and solemn. Our friends Mr. and Mrs. Bogart welcomed us cordially into the church. This was a most important step in our life, and we have always been glad we took it, and that we had the opportunity of bringing up our children in the Church. I was twenty-seven and your father thirty-four years of age.

On Lucy's birthday, when she was five years old, April 13th, 1861, was fired at Ft. Sumter, South Carolina, the first gun of the War Between the States. We heard the reports of the cannon all day in Savannah. It was Saturday. In the afternoon I took Lucy to walk and heard from some of my friends on the streets that we were victorious. This news inspired our people. Men organized themselves into companies, and war was declared. Your father, full of patriotism, volunteered at once, and was appointed 2nd Lieutenant in a Company under Captain Reed. These were sad days for me. He was a handsome soldier with his gray uniform, red sash, and handsome sword. He made his arrangements to go to Virginia with this company and resigned his place in the Academy. On May 31st, a Friday afternoon, before going, we had our three little daughters baptized in St. John's Church by Reverend Mr. Clark. Little Alice was ten months old. Belle held her in her arms. Lucy was five and Cornelia three.

The Company was to leave the last of June, but I was so heartbroken that your father gratified me by resigning. Knowing him as I do, I know what an effort this cost him. He sold his sash to the officer elected in his place and his sword to the Captain. The sword was broken in two on the battle field, and the Lieutenant wearing his sash was killed that summer in Virginia. It was feared that the enemy would attack Fort Pulaski that Spring. He, Mr. Bogart, and Mr. Lancaster, teachers in the Academy, went with the Chatham Artillery, I think it was, to assist in defending the Fort. He carried a cot, bedclothing, and a trunk to make himself comfortable, which comforts he did not have during the latter part of the War. Fort Pulaski was on the Savannah River. The enemy did not attack it.

During the month of June, there was a good deal of scarlet fever in Savannah, and our dear little Alice was taken ill one day and died the next morning in my lap. This was the first time I had faced death, and we were in great distress. She died the 22nd of June, 1861, three weeks from the day she was baptized. We concluded she must have had the scarlet fever, though the physician did not say so. Your father bought a beautiful little rosewood casket, and many friends came to us. That afternoon, because it was Saturday and a very hot day and she had died of a malignant disease, she was buried in a lot your father bought in Laurel Grove Cemetery. I have the deed to this lot now. The funeral was held at the house. Rev. Mr. Pryse officiated, as our Rector had gone north. I robed the little baby myself in the dress in which she was baptized. My friends wanted to do it, but I begged to be allowed to do it. I also wrote a letter to Mother that day telling her of our great trouble. This was the first shadow that had crossed our threshold. Soon after I left for Jonesville.

Your father had, in the meantime, joined an engineering corps, and after I left he went to the Island of Sapelo and was entertained by Mr. Randolph Spaulding, who owned the greater part of the island. Captain Miller Grant had charge of the work of throwing up fortifications. Your father assisted him. He spent the time very pleasantly there; he had studied Civil Engineering. He joined me the 1st of September and leaving the children with their grandmother, we went to Savannah and stored away all of our furniture in two rooms in Chatham Academy, thus breaking up our home. I gathered together the most precious things we had and took them out to Liberty with me, among them the bronze clock which I now have, and which you all have seen, also a pair of vases which I now use. These things have now been in my possession forty-two years.

The first dreadful battle of Manassas had occurred in June in which so many of our soldiers were killed, among them Colonel Barton of Savannah. In October, your father bade us good-by and left for Savannah where he joined the Chatham Artillery under Captain Cleghorn and spent the winter of 1861 and 1862 on the Isle of Hope as a private soldier. We moved to the plantation, and it was a sad winter for me. My little girls and your father's frequent letters, together with the kindness of my dear father and mother, cheered me. I was very comfortable in their large house with plenty of servants. We had not begun to feel the privations yet of the War. We got the mail three times a week. Your father had an ambrotype taken of himself at about this time, which was considered good, and I have it still. He wrote very cheerfully, expecting the yankees at any time, but they never came. I do not remember of his having but one furlough during that winter, and it was of only a few days' length. Sister was living at home, and Sam and Mary were living at their plantation, Cedar Hill. The servants were not demoralized yet, and things moved peacefully along.

When I could, I attended services at old Midway. The young men from all over the county had volunteered and were in service. So only old gentlemen and youths were to be seen in the congregation. Sam was such a sufferer from asthma that he did not volunteer at first, and Father was nearly sixty. In July of that year, 1862, President Davis issued an order that soldiers thirty-five years and older were not required to be in service, so your father resigned his place, wishing to change his manner of serving his country. He came out to Jonesville and spent about two months with us, then went to Savannah and joined Captain McReady's Engineering Corps stationed at the Isle of Hope. This work was more suitable to his taste. He occupied a room in Savannah over a book store with his friend, Daniel Alcott, driving out each day to attend to his work on the Island. This was a pleasant winter for both him and us, as he was in no danger.

I made him two visits, once in December and once in February, leaving the children with their grandmother. The first visit, he took me to the Pavillion Hotel and the next to the Screven House. I had my teeth attended to, and he also took me out to the Isle of Hope. He had an Irish woman to roast oysters for us, and he enjoyed handing them to me on the half shell. She seemed to enjoy our happiness and merriment, and I have never forgotten her. I wish I could remember her name. I don't suppose she had seen a man so courtly to his wife before. I found Savannah very much changed. There was very little in the stores. I found it difficult to get shoes. I met some of my old friends. We spent one evening with Mr. and Mrs. Bogart, quite a long walk for me from the Screven House to Taylor Street.

Before I go further, I must tell you that your father gave me, in 1860, one of the first sewing machines that were made, a Wheeler and Wilson. I took it out to Liberty with me, but sewed very little on it, because I had very little cloth to sew. Your grandfather Pond sent me several times, bolts of unbleached domestic that were woven in the factories at Columbus. Mother had a spinning wheel upon which Nellie spun yarn of cotton grown on the plantation and out of which we knitted socks, and even stockings for ourselves and the little girls. Our knitting needles were never idle except on Sunday. I knitted all the socks that your father wore during the War. Then my father got a loom and Nellie wove cloth to make clothes for the negroes. He bought large bales of yarn from the factories for this purpose. I learned to prepare the warp on a frame for the loom and put it through the eyes of the harness and through the sley and would often try to weave, but had hardly strength to do it. Mother had a reel upon which she would put a skein of yarn and wind it in a ball. All of this was new work to us.

From our friends on the coast, we got the long-leaf palmetto, a yard and a half long, and stripped it into fine strips and plaited braids for hats, both for ourselves, my little girls, and the gentlemen of the family. We learned several kinds of plaits. Even little Lucy and Cornelia plaited with their little fingers. We made the braids into hats. I had Cudjo our carpenter to make me two blocks the size of my head, and the little girls, upon which I put the hats and pressed them into shape. We also made dyes from the barks of different trees and bushes. Of sweet gum bark we made a gray dye, gallberry a black, and walnut, a brown. Copperas and alum we used as mordants and set the colors. We dyed some of the straw black, and made black hats or mixed it with the white straw. We dyed our thread gray to make our dresses sometimes, grey and white plaids sometimes. We made blacking for shoes by boiling the chinaberries and skimming off the oil and mixing it with soot. I learned to knit gloves, both with fingers and without.

Mother made candles from the myrtle berries by boiling them and skimming off the grease and putting it in moulds. This made pretty blue candles, giving a good light. She also made tallow candles made from the tallow of Father's bees. She also burned lard in a large lamp that she had and found that it made beautiful light.

You must know that your grandfather raised a great many hogs, cured his own bacon, and boasted that he never bought a ham until he left Liberty County. He also had a larger number of cattle, cows and sheep, and we lived mostly on what was raised on the farm. Mother raised a great many turkeys, chickens, and ducks. Four fattening-coops were always filled, ready for use. Eggs were plentiful. The dairy was in the yard with shelves filled with pans of milk. Zog, the house boy, was daily seen churning, or beating rice in the yard. Father planted largely in rice, sea island cotton, sweet potatoes, corn, peas, etc. He shipped his rice and cotton to Savannah on a schooner that came up the Riceboro River. He had a gin house where he ginned his own cotton and packed it in bales for the market. He also had a cotton house with a large scaffold, a floor on high poles upon which the fleecy staple was dried.

When the rice was cut in the fall it was brought in from the field and stacked in large stacks in the rice yard. On a bright, windy day in winter, you could hear the negro men threshing out the rice with their flails. Then it would be taken up into a high house called the "winnowing house." They would throw it down, and the wind would blow away the straw. Then it would be carried into a large barn nearby where Father always had thousands of bushels. It was then ready for the market and was called "rough rice." This was what Zog beat in a large wooden mortar with a wooden pestle every day, fanning off the chaff until it was clean and white for use. Then on other days it would be washed and beaten in the mortar into rice flour, from which we made waffles, egg bread, fritters, etc.

Father always made abundant crops of corn from which we had meal and hominy. He always said he made more corn each year than he needed for his family, negroes, and stock. He was proud of this, thinking a planter who had to buy corn before the year was out was a very poor manager. It was the custom every Monday night for the negroes to collect around the corn house door to receive their rations for the week, dispensed by the "driver" (over-seer).

Your grandfather had gotten some tea plants before the War from his cousin Senator Alfred Iverson in Washington. They had grown up into large bushes by this time, and he made his own tea from the tender leaves. They were picked from the bushes in the afternoon and spread on a table to wilt. The next morning they were rolled between the palms of the hands, then put in the oven, moderately warm and dried. My little daughters and I have often helped pick the leaves, and I helped make the tea.

Father also planted wheat during the War and had it ground in the upper part of the county. This was a new departure for him as he had always bought flour in Savannah by the barrel. Sugar and coffee were now very high. They were the only things he had to buy, and they were hard to get. He had a large supply of Java coffee on hand when the War commenced, but it gave out at length. He never would consent to try the substitutes others used and recommended such as sweet potatoes sliced raw and parched, and dried okra seed parched. We even made some of our own medicines. For instance, opium from the seed vessels of the single poppy. Incisions were made in the green seed vessels in the afternoon from which a milk would exude. The next morning we would scrape it off on little plates. This would harden and make the real unadulterated opium. Medicines were very scarce and expensive. Our ports were blockaded, and we could not buy anything from foreign countries unless a ship ran the blockade. So the South had to depend upon what she made herself to feed and clothe her citizens and her soldiers.

Brother [William Louis Jones] was engaged by the Government to make gun powder near Augusta, Georgia. We used Confederate money which, as the War advanced, depreciated very much in value, paying enormous prices for ordinary things. This is now the Spring of 1863. Sister had engaged herself to Captain Benjamin Screven the fall before, and they were married on the 25th of June. Father gave her $400.00, and I remember how few things she was able to get. On the 3rd of June we were blessed with "another sweet little daughter" whom we named "Eloise Thomas." Your father came out unexpectedly on the 2nd of June and so fortunately was with me at that time. She was a very lovely, healthy baby and very warmly welcomed by us all, especially by her two little sisters. She was born in the room at the plantation in which I was born twenty-nine years before. I have always said that we had a "Daughter of the Confederacy" too. Your father was only able to stay ten days when he was ordered to Tennessee by the Nitre and Mining Bureau under Dr. Nathaniel Pratt. He superintended the works there near Charlestown on the Hiawassee River. In his letters he describes this country as beautiful with everything in abundance, before the northern army invaded it.

I must now tell you about your Aunt Rosa's wedding. As it was a "War wedding," it was a very different affair from mine. The ceremony was performed in the parlor of our dear old plantation home by our cousin, the Rev. Richard Way, who had returned from China. Only a few persons were present, the immediate members of both families. My two little daughters, little Lula and little Sissie as we called them, were her only attendants. The bride was dressed in a simple white organdie dress and looked very sweet. Captain Screven wore his Confederate uniform of gray. The wedding took place at 9 o'clock in the morning.

Although it was War times, we had delightful refreshments; delicious cake, syllabub and gelatine, and custard were passed around. Sam and I had a great deal of fun together. His wife and little Lila were just recovering from an attack of sickness and could not come. Captain Screven was a widower, and his sister Mrs. Mallard was present with his three little sons, the oldest about nine years old. Cousin Susan Way, the minister's wife, was also present; these were all the guests.

That night after supper, Captain Screven's Company, cavalry, rode over to the plantation to congratulate him and his bride. They fired their salutes on the lawn; then Father and Captain Screven went out to meet them. Lieutenant John Baker made a graceful congratulatory speech to his Captain to which Captain Screven responded. Then my father invited the Company in to supper. They were conducted into the dining room where they enjoyed a bountiful repast consisting of turkey, ham, ducks, and chickens, breads, cakes, boiled custard, syllabub etc. This was a very great treat to the soldiers, such a change from their army fare.

As no ladies were present, I remember they gave way to their mirth, singing war songs. One I remember: "The girl I left behind me." I was in the shed-room peeping at them through a crack in the door. We gave them plenty of sweet milk, and they seemed glad to get it. They made speeches and gave toasts, although there was no wine or anything intoxicating to drink as Father was a strictly temperate man. Some of the officers requested to see the bride, to pay their respects to her, and they were taken to the parlor. While I was peeping through the door, I felt someone pulling at my dress—it was Father telling me to go upstairs to my baby, who was crying very loudly.

We moved to Jonesville July 1st. Sister spent the summer with us there while the Captain returned to camp near Sunbury. It was during this month that the great battle of Gettysburg was fought, with terrible disaster to our arms. Your father remained in Tennessee until September when the Federal army approaching, he had to pack the Confederate stores in wagons and escape to Dalton, Georgia, with them. From thence he came down to see me, arriving on the 19th of September. This ended his work in that line. In October, Col. J.M.B. Millen of Savannah organized a regiment and appointed your father as his adjutant with the rank of Captain. I was very glad to have him so near home as he was stationed near Sunbury. In the early fall they moved to Riceboro, just three miles from the plantation. Father gave him a fine bay mare costing $1,000, named Katie, of whom he was very proud.

That winter of '63 and '64 was one of the most pleasant to us during the War. He rode over frequently to see us, looking very handsome in his Confederate uniform. Father invited Colonel

Millen and his staff and Captain Screven to take dinner with him on Christmas Day. This was a fine dinner too, for we still had plenty of poultry and hams, milk and butter, and cream for syllabub, not yet having felt the privations of war except having to wear such plain clothing. This Christmas I told my little girls that on account of the War, Santa Claus was so poor that he could not bring them any dolls or toys. So all they found Christmas morning were little cakes, hardboiled eggs, and sugar cane. But they fully understood the hard times and were very happy.

The latter part of March 1864 orders came for the regiment to be sent to Virginia, the seat of war. This struck terror to my heart. Very soon it was on the march. When it would make a long stop as at Savannah or Augusta, your father would come back on horseback to see us, thinking probably he would never see us again. He also went to Columbus to see his parents. The battalion reached Richmond the last week in May, and Saturday, the 28th of May, was in a battle at Hawes' Shop above Richmond. In this, Colonel Millen was killed—shot through the head, Captain Screven shot through the wind pipe, and quite a number were killed and wounded. Your father was not touched although in the thickest of the fight.

The next battle he was in was at Trevellian Station. When he came out of the battle he found that Katie, his horse, had been killed. He thought he had put her in a safe place, but she had been killed and robbed. It was some time before he could get another horse. He was in many battles that summer, seventeen in all, and was never hit, save once by a spent ball. He was often in very dangerous places. I received frequent letters from him. I was kept in a constant state of suspense. It was a very unhappy summer. I have these interesting letters still.

In the fall he was transferred to the 10th Georgia Regiment under Colonel Taliaferro—the 20th battalion having been disbanded—was so cut up and its colonel killed. The 26th of November, 1864, I received the last letter that he wrote from Virginia and heard no more from him until he suddenly appeared April 4th, 1865. Communication had been entirely cut off by Sherman's march through Georgia and the Carolinas.

The winter of '64 and '65 was a terrible one to us. Rumors came that Sherman's army was coming through Georgia burning and devastating the country, of horrible treatment of old men and ladies, and finally we heard that he had reached Savannah. General Kilpatrick's division came out to Liberty and encamped at Midway Church, eight miles from Father's plantation. They sent out daily foraging parties. On the morning of December 15th, 1864, a squad of twelve or fifteen yankee soldiers in their dark blue uniforms galloped through the front gate, through the lawn, and around to the stables, whooping and hallooing. A number of the negro men came from the quarters and greeted them. We could see them whispering and asking questions. Father had had all his horses and mules put in a pen in the woods far off from the house to save them. But these negroes piloted them to the spot. Very soon we had to see the yankees returning with them.

Father had spent several nights in the woods for fear of being taken prisoner and to escape the terrible treatment said to be inflicted on old gentlemen. They were often hung up by their thumbs to force them to tell where their money was. Sam, who had been in the hospital service at Columbia, S.C., was now making us a visit with his wife and little daughter. He was recovering from a severe attack of erysipelas and was still confined to his bed upstairs. We were terrified lest they should come in and take him prisoner in his weak condition. Some of the yankees came into the house, walking into rooms without knocking, hunting for silver and firearms, watches, jewelry, and money, besides food. They inquired of the negroes where my father was, and they told them to tell him to come home, that they would not trouble him. So he did, much to our delight. They took off that day all the wagons, buggies, and the rockaway. They did not take the large family carriage. The smokehouse was filled with meat, as Father had killed hogs the week before.

That night, we ladies sat up all night, not taking off our clothing. After midnight, having fallen asleep, we were aroused by Father's saying, "Wake up, hundreds of yankees are coming and are at the negro houses now." They were on their way to the Altamaha River to burn the railroad bridge, and a large detachment had come to get corn. Father asked the officer for a guard to protect the house. This he granted, but it did not prevent the rabble from coming in. A rough crowd poured through the house, going through the rooms, searching every bureau, wardrobe, closets, and trunks. They took all the silverware and jewelry that we had not hidden and everything to eat that could be found.

A squad came to the back steps and asked for whiskey or brandy. Father replied that there was none in the house. Poor Mother, remembering a demijon of wine in poor sick Sam's room, said, "Oh, Mr. Jones, you've forgotten the demijohn of wine in poor sick Sam's room." "Where is Sam's room?," we heard them shout. We thought they were going to take our poor weak brother prisoner. Father led the way upstairs, poor Mother following close behind. Soon we heard another shout as they found the wine, and then we heard them tramping downstairs. Our minds were soon relieved when we heard they had not troubled Sam and only wanted the wine.

That night they searched and robbed the house of everything they wanted. To their credit, I will say that they left my room unmolested, merely opening the door without knocking, and seeing us ladies would retire. None of us retired that night. We were afraid to do so. The next morning my mother's beautifully kept home was a scene of disorder and desolation. The dining table was stripped of everything. Table cloth, napkins, china, and silver were gone. The drawers of Father's secretary were taken out and lying on the floor, rifled, the sideboard robbed of everything, closets and pantry doors wide open, with nothing left in them, as preserves, pickles, etc. In the bedrooms, the bureaus were searched, drawers lying on the floor.

When we went out on the back piazza, no sign of life anywhere. The hen houses and fattening coops had been emptied of all the poultry, the smoke house and store room doors and dairy were wide open and robbed of everything. The hog pens were empty and not a fowl, goose, turkey or duck to be seen anywhere. The kitchen door was standing open, and no breakfast cooking. Imagine our despair. About 150 negroes in 100 yards of the house, idle and demoralized. We still had our negro nurses, girls about fifteen years, who slept in the house, to help us.

We looked around to see what we could find to cook and eat. There were eleven of us in all, besides the three nurses. After searching, a little meal, a small piece of side of bacon, and some lard and salt were found. These we took upstairs and put in a market basket and hid in the garret. We cooked what little we ate in the fireplace in my room for three weeks. Father's corn house still held a great deal of corn after they had taken what they wanted. The rice house was full of rough rice, so we did not fear starvation, and there were also a plenty of peas.

For three weeks, squads of soldiers came and took what they wanted, filling their "pokes" (bags), as they called them, with corn. One day, I watched one of them trying to shoot a pig that had been left, and he was such a poor marksman, I thought, if all of them were as poor shots, our soldiers had nothing to fear. One morning, we tried to cook on the fireplace in a vacant room opposite to mine. No sooner was the breakfast done than to our dismay some of them rudely entered and took everything that was prepared, with a shout. We did not attempt to cook anything more that day.

During the afternoon, two of the lowest and roughest of the soldiers came into the house calling each other "captain" and "colonel," saying that there were five watches in the house, and they intended to have them, that every room had been searched but mine, and they wanted the ladies to leave the room. They were in one of the front rooms upstairs searching alone with Father when they said this. So he came to my room and asked us what we would do. We decided to remain in the room. Upon Father's telling them our reply they said, "Very well, we will burn the house down." Father turned around, locked the door, put the key in his pocket saying, "Very well, we can die but once, we will all die together." One of them asked Father for a match; he gave it to him, whereupon the yankee pretended to ignite a muslin dress hanging in the room, then turning to Father, said, "If it were not for that sick man in the other room, I would do it anyhow." What a kind, tender-hearted, cowardly yankee!

Soon they entered my room followed by Father and Mother. We watched them contemptuously. They searched the bureau drawers, but fortunately, failing to take them out and lay them on the floor, they did not see the thick overcoat of Father's which I had hidden in the little shallow drawer within the bottom of the bureau without any handles. Imagine my delight when I saw them leave the bureau and knew that I had outwitted that yankee.

Sam's overcoat, which was hanging in my closet, had been stolen a few days before. Mother, meeting the soldier coming down stairs with it, entreated him to give her back her poor sick son's overcoat. He uttered a terrible oath and walked off with it. This would-be "colonel" and "captain" crawled under the beds searching, shook the mattresses to see if silverware were hidden in them, then gave a terrible shout as they found a little meal and a little jar of lard in a box, and a little piece of bacon which we had secreted behind the bed. You would have thought they had found a great treasure.

Poor Mother's underclothing had been handled so often by them in searching the bureau drawers in her room, that she had to put them in a springlock trunk and sent it up to my room. They at once thought that that trunk held the hidden treasure. They asked her for the key, she said the key was lost, so the "captain" asked the "colonel" if he could not open it with his sword. "O yes, Captain," said the "colonel." Mother protested that the trunk contained only an old lady's underclothing. They would not believe her and soon picked the lock with the sword and found nothing else. I shall never forget that scene. Even Lucy, who was then eight years old, remembers it distinctly. They went out of the room empty-handed, finding nothing.

A few days before this, this "captain and colonel" had found the opening into the garret and insisted upon going up there.

They mounted a table and pushing aside the trap door, went up. They spied the market basket I have mentioned and shouted as if it contained gold. They did not take the groceries, however, but searched the garret well. While they were searching my room, Father asked one, "Are you not the same man who searched my garret a day or so ago?" "I am the boy," he replied.

Another day these same men returned and sent insulting notes to the house to us ladies by one of the oldest servants, George. Father and Mother never let us know of these notes till sometime afterwards. Upon Father refusing to deliver the notes and comply with their request, they threatened to burn the house. His reply was "Burn it!" Soon they saw George with a large lighted torch coming toward the house with the men on horseback behind him as if they were driving him forward. Mother was terrified, but Father did not know what fear was. Suddenly, they saw George drop the torch and the two yankees wheel their horses around and gallop out of the enclosure. They had seen a squad of their own soldiers coming from the opposite direction. They had come for corn. Father told them of the conduct of the two soldiers, and they said they would report them at camp, but we doubted if it was ever done.

One night a squad of them camped all night on our lawn and got our fine old cook, Chloe, to cook for them. She told me afterwards, "Why Miss Nela, I t'ought a yankee was lak de debbul, but de ones I cooked fer, wuz as nice genelmens as I ebber saw." One of the soldiers saw his father's name, "Gilbert," on Father's wagon, and upon inquiry, found Father had always bought them from his father's factory in Hartford, Connecticut. He then seemed to take an interest in us and gave Father some real ground coffee, which was the first we had seen in a long time. We drank it, but some of us were afraid to do so.

He also gave little Eloise, then about eighteen months old, a silver quarter which I wore in my shoe until the yankees left the county. This little tot would often run to me and say, "Yankee tum, Yankee tum."

To save Sam's clothing while he was in bed (fearing he would be taken prisoner and all his clothing stolen), I wore his shoes over mine for some time, and Sister and his wife wore his underclothing strapped around them under their clothes. We had very little to eat during this time that was appetizing, and one day a negro man named Raymond, who had married one of Father's negro women and who did not live on the plantation, brought us a fat hen nicely baked. That day three yankees came into my room and commenced talking with us. The hen was in a tin pan, and I had put it under my chair, and drawing my full skirts around it, so saved it. They asked the usual question, "What time of day is it?," thinking we would look at our watches and they would take them. But we had them hidden in the woods, of which I will tell you afterwards.

One cold afternoon about sunset, when we hoped they had gone back to camp for the night, this same Mr. Gilbert came back bringing a Confederate soldier, a prisoner. This excited us very much. He asked Father if he could keep him there that night. We were so sorry for the poor soldier. Father could get very little information from him except that he belonged to Wheeler's Cavalry. Father never believed he was a Confederate soldier. Mother had to let them sleep in one of her beds, and we had to cook for them and share our scanty meals with them. The next morning Mother took the sheets and pillow cases into my room to save them, and I saw that they were full of "gray backs" (lice), the first I ever saw.

This year, Christmas Day came on Sunday. Never did we

spend as dreary a one. The house was so bare and comfortless. Santa Claus would not come to make the little children happy. No Christmas turkey or anything. The little children thought that the yankees would not let Santa Claus come.

The last week in December, one afternoon about sunset, Father received a note from his niece Laura Jones, who was now the wife of Major Camp of the Confederate Army, saying they had been subjected to such insults that day that she and her sisters, Leonora, then the widow of Captain Rush McConnell, and Rosa, a young girl, were afraid to remain at their plantation another night. She asked if they could not come to Father's until they could refugee to southwest Georgia. Father was glad to have them, of course. So that night about nine o'clock, Laura and her sisters and their children (Laura's little son, Augustus, and Leonora's little girl, Laurella, and their fourteen year old brother, Clifford) walking, arrived at our plantation. They came under a yankee guard. Laura had difficulty in keeping Clifford from talking defiantly to the yankees. Leonora had their silver spoons, knives, and forks in a bundle tied around her waist under her clothes, and she was very much afraid the guard would hear them rattling as she walked. We were delighted to have them with us, and they told us of their experiences, the same we had had, the same insults received from the same "colonel and captain." They brought a dressed guinea with them which we all enjoyed the next day. They left their house, nicely furnished, and everything they had, to the mercy of the negroes, yankees, and "crackers," who completely stripped the house of everything.

Colonel Arthur Hood had obtained permission from the yankee commander at Midway to allow him to conduct women and children and noncombatants through the lines across the

Altamaha River, Saturday morning, the 31st of December, 1864. Colonel Hood, accompanied by a yankee guard, and with a large wagon, came to our plantation and these ladies and Sister and her little baby Rosalie, her maid Eliza and her baby, Patsy, Sam's wife Mary, and their little daughter Lila, four years old, went with them. Mary's and Sister's nurses Elsie and Bess, young girls, hid and could not be found at the last moment, and they had to go without them. Cousin Jane LeConte Harden's two daughters, Mrs. Annie Adams and Ada Harden, joined them at their home on the road. They reached Walthourville that night and camped in a vacant house, the village being almost deserted.

It was not considered safe for Sam to travel with them in the daytime, so after dark, still weak from his long illness, he got on a lame "Sally mule" of Father's that the yankees had left, and accompanied by our faithful servant, Peter, he set out for Walthourville. They were afraid to take the big road which passed by the negro houses (our own negroes—Peter did not want them to see him, either, taking Sam away!); they went through the woods and fields and entered the road beyond the negro houses. Afraid of our own negroes telling on him! They joined Cousin Joseph LeConte and Cousin Jane's faithful servant Billy. They spent the night at Walthourville. The next day, they all proceeded on their way to the Altamaha, crossed the lines and went down to southwest Georgia. I remained at the plantation with Father and Mother and my three little children. We thought we would follow the others soon, but Sherman's army soon after left the county, proceeding its way through the Carolinas to Richmond. Father decided to remain at home and protect his property.

This was a very sad New Year to us. It was a long time before we ever set the table and ate as we used to do. I would fix their plates and take them to Father and Mother as they sat on each side of the sitting room fireplace. Mother kept looking out the window fearing the yankees' return, although assured that they had left the county. Father was very much dejected and often said that he had lost the work of forty years. He seemed to me to have aged ten years in those three weeks. Nellie, our faithful seamstress, continued faithful and helped us by cooking dinner at her house and bringing it to us. We had plenty of corn and peas and rice left. Father had his cows driven up, and we soon had milk and butter. Some of the pigs were found left in the woods, and some of the sheep too, and we began to have a plenty to eat again, though no luxuries. One day an old hen appeared, only one had escaped, and Mother called her "Jennie" for herself.

It was now February that Father decided to go into the woods and bring back a valise and a box in which valuables had been hidden. He had only permitted one man, the most faithful and honest, he thought, except Peter, to help him bury them. He did this so that if anything happened to him, Fortune would know where to find them. Father went alone first, and to his astonishment both had been removed. In the valise were Father's gold watch and chain, your father's watch and chain, Mary and Sam's gold watch and chain, which had belonged to her father, her jewelry, the gold medallion containing your father's picture, his seal ring, and valuable papers of Father's. In the box was the silver plate belonging to Sam and Mary. Father then called Fortune and told him to go and bring them, not letting him know that he had been. Fortune returned saying they were gone. Father then found, to his great surprise, that his "faithful" servant had betrayed him. I am glad to tell you that they were afterwards recovered, and all was safe except your father's watch. That and his seal ring, and all of Mary's jewelry and her watch, had been taken. The silver was untouched.

A searching party of negroes looked all day, Fortune at their head, and finally "found" the valise and box in the woods. This was all a pretense as they had been taken to the negro houses and divided out, and then hidden them again. One of the negroes, Frank, had Father's watch and chain, but he had brought it to Father the night before. Sam had come home in February on a visit and had frightened them assembled around the back door the night before by firing off his pistol over their heads and saying he would not put up with their stealing his wife's property, and they must bring it back. This caused Frank to bring Father's watch back and caused the searching party the next day. The negroes said Paul (the boy who used to go to school with me) had your father's watch and chain, and as he had been shot and killed on the Darien road, I never recovered it. I had appealed to Fortune many times to bring me back the medallion containing Mr. Pond's picture, saying that if he were ever killed in the War, his little children would never know how their father looked. When the valise was returned it was in it, so I suppose I touched his heart. He used to declare his innocence saying, "Pore eenicent Fortin don know no mo 'bout it dan de babe unbawn!"

Lambright, the carriage-driver, brought back the hat box (a small trunk) that I had intrusted to him and some saddles of Father's, and Peter brought back what had been intrusted to him and Andrew, one of Captain Screven's servants, brought back the trunk Sister had given him to hide. These men were honest and did not have to be threatened. Sister buried Captain Screven's watch and chain in a little box in the hen house, and it was saved. The only thing Mother had hidden was her silver soup ladle, which she hid in an enormous hedge in the side garden. One day after the yankees were gone, she went to look for it, and found it safe, to our surprise. She gave it to me in after years, and we use it still. I could have saved your father's watch if I had hidden it on my person.

This winter passed away in a sad and lonely manner. We could get no mail but heard from an occasional passerby of the march of Sherman's army through the Carolinas, burning everything as he went. Your father, as I heard from him afterwards, was with Hampton's Cavalry at Columbia, S.C., when Sherman's army marched in and burned the city. They had to retreat before him. I was still ignorant of his whereabouts, or if he were still alive.

After the army had left Midway, the negro men went to the camp and brought back broken-down horses. Peter brought back Sam's elegant black horse Old Black, completely broken down. He came up to the gate of the yard where we were standing, instead of following Peter to the stable, and looked at us as if he were glad to get home again. We welcomed him back, but in spite of all our care of him, he died soon from the hard usage he had received. We never saw any of our other horses again though many were brought back to the county.

Things seemed now to have come to a standstill. People who had refugeed began to return to their homes. They found their elegant homes stripped of everything, their barns empty, and all signs of life gone from their plantations, except their idle lazy negroes. Father was then glad that he had remained at home and so saved his home and its contents. Many people returned to find their dwelling houses in ashes. Our summer home in Jonesville was burned. We never knew who did it.

Aunt Harriet Quarterman and Mrs. John Barnard each left their homes, handsomely furnished throughout. Mrs. Barnard returned to find hers in ashes and Aunt Harriet, hers in Walthourville completely stripped of everything. This was the experience of many others.

The winter passed drearily and slowly away. On the 3rd of April, 1865, Leonora McConnell, my cousin, came back from southwest Georgia to see about her deserted home and to see if anything was left in the house. She spent a few days with us. She had heard that their overseer had carried off their furniture to his home in the piney woods. On the morning of the 4th, she and I went in the wagon in which she had come, with Lambright and her former servant Amos, to the overseer's to try to recover the furniture if possible. When we went into his house, she saw their sideboard, chairs, bedroom furniture, etc. Leonora showed such tact. She would say, "Why here is our sideboard. I am so obliged to you for taking care of it for us, and keeping the negroes from stealing it." And hearing of a sick man in the next room she asked to be allowed to go in to see if she could do anything for him. Her object was to see what was in the room of hers. The bed the man was lying on belonged to her family. The overseer could do nothing but give them up when she approached him in this manner, and soon Lambright and Amos had the wagon loaded with the recovered articles.

On our return home, we were met by one of Father's little negro boys, Caesar, who told us that Mr. Pond had come home. We could not believe it, but he insisted it was true, saying "he had on soldier's clothes and was on horseback." I was wild with joy and excitement, and Leonora said I pinched and squeezed her all the way home, saying I could not believe it. It was too good to be true. I had not heard from him in more than four months and had not seen him for eleven months. When we drove in sight of the house, there he was sitting on the steps of the porch with Father. He hurried out to meet us and literally lifted me out of the wagon! In spite of all his hardships, he looked well and handsome. He told me he had only come home on a furlough to get recruits. On the following Sunday, April the 9th, 1865, General Lee surrendered, and he never left home again.

When he rode up to the house, he saw no one. He walked back to the dining room expecting to see the family there. Instead, there sat Nellie at the loom weaving. She exclaimed, "Why, Mr. Pond!" He asked where was everybody, and she directed him to the sitting room. When he opened the door he saw Father and Mother and his little children sitting at the table. Everything had been changed. Mother exclaimed, "Why, Thomas!," and they were all so glad to welcome him home. I had not been away from home in a year, and to think I was not home to welcome him. It was so unfortunate. I had citizen's clothing and underclothing saved for him, and he very soon asked me for a bath and some clean clothes, which I had immediately prepared for him. He brought nothing back but the clothes he had on and four brown blankets. For months he had washed his underclothing and put them on damp. He had only a change. When he rejoined us after his refreshing bath, he looked so natural and nice in his black clothes and white linen. I picked up his underclothing with the tongs and gave them to a woman to wash immediately.

One day Pratt and Emma Quarterman came from Jonesville to see us and told us that General Robert Lee had surrendered and that the soldiers were returning by Walthourville. My

father would not believe it. He insisted it was General Fitz-
hugh Lee and not General Robert E. Lee. But finally we were
obliged to believe it. Though regretting our defeat, I rejoiced
that the War was over and that my husband was safe at home,
having passed through many battles untouched. He had come
home on horseback. As he came through South Carolina, an
old gentleman had given him a beautiful black pony named
Johnny Reb, saying as he gave it, "I know that Sherman's army
will take him from me, and I prefer him to be owned by one of
our own soldiers." So your father rode on his own horse, Bob,
a large sorrel, and led Johnny Reb all the way from Columbia,
South Carolina, through Augusta, Georgia, down to Liberty
County. We had much to tell of our experiences, he of long
marches on horseback, sometimes falling asleep, once losing
his cap, of often sleeping on the cold bare ground with his
saddle for a pillow, of often being so hungry that once he picked
up a piece of cornbread lying by the side of the road and ate it.
Everything was so dear. Confederate money was of very little
value. He had to give $2.00 a quart for sweet milk, $6.00 for a
chicken, and everything else in proportion. I have his letters
describing his war experiences which you children can read.

He had been very uneasy about us knowing that Sherman's
army had been through the county. His indignation knew no
bounds as I would relate to him the indignities which we had
suffered. Mother told him that one day when she was quite sick
in bed with sore throat and fever, the yankees came in and out
of her room all day without knocking. One young man was
busily ransacking her bureau drawers when she asked him,
"How would you like your mother's clothing handled as you
are doing mine?" He uttered an oath and said, "I never had a
mother!" This so shocked her that she said she never spoke an-

other word to any of them. I often think of the picture of the old lady lying there in her night cap pleading with that rough young soldier. One day she and Sister were on the back piazza when two rode up, cursed them in a shocking manner without any reason, then wheeled their horses and cantered away, leaving them in horrified speechlessness. Such profanity had never been heard by us before.

About the last of April, to our surprise, one day Captain Screven and Sister, with their little Rosalie and her faithful servant Eliza and her baby, arrived in Mrs. Roswell King's carriage from Taylors Creek. They had come from Augusta in an ambulance to that place. Sister had a varied experience, having gone first to Thomas County, then to Baker, then to Early, visiting relatives, from thence through Albany to Augusta where she met the Captain returning from the War. We were delighted to see them and she to get back. She regretted ever having gone. She never would have gone, but she had thought that we would soon follow her and break up the old home.

STARTING OVER
IN A NEW SOUTH

"We left the dear old county for good."

About this time the negroes agreed to work and make a crop, and Father agreed to give them a certain proportion, so the plantation settled down to work again. Mr. Pond's two horses were put in the plows, and he helped in every way he could. Never before had the horses been locked up at night, but now, locks had to be put on the stables because the negroes were now free and lawless. During the winter they could be seen walking the road in yankee overcoats with guns on their shoulders, a sight unknown in slavery times.

Now for the first time we began to know fear of those who formerly had been our protectors. Captain Screven found that his double buggy had not been taken by the yankees because it was out of repair. This he brought to the plantation, and with Bob and Johnnie Reb, we now had a nice turnout. This Spring your father had to go all the way to Thomasville on horseback to take the oath of allegiance. This was a bitter pill to him and to every Confederate soldier. Carroll Varnedoe went with him. They had a hard time crossing the Altamaha River as the bridge was burned. I have that paper with the oath signed by him, containing a description of him, his age, height, and complexion, etc.

News came to us about the last of April of the assassination of Lincoln, by J. Wilkes Booth at the theatre in Washington City. On Good Friday night, April 14th, Lincoln was in a box with his wife and friends. Booth entered the box, shot Lincoln, then leaped down upon the stage. His foot caught in a United States Flag, he fell, hurting his ankle. Brandishing his weapon he shouted, "Sic semper tyrannis!," rushed out of the back of the theatre, sprang on his horse, and escaped. Lincoln was carried home and died. Booth was afterwards captured in a barn in Virginia and was killed. We thought we had been delivered from our worst enemy. It was he and his Republican party who brought on the War, it was he who had issued the emancipation proclamation Jan. 1st, 1863, which had freed our negroes. But we found out in after years that if he had lived, the South might have been paid for her negroes and that his death was a misfortune to the South.

We had no opportunity of seeing any newspapers as the railroad (S.F.& W.) was destroyed from Savannah across the Altamaha bridge. This was a great loss to the state. So we did not know in what a state of excitement the country was. A detachment of General Wilson's army, which raided through Alabama at the same time that Sherman was coming through Georgia, reached Columbus, Georgia where our relatives lived,

Easter day April 16th. They did not do any damage to the town as the War was over. But that day, your venerable grandfather Pond was walking on the streets when he met a young yankee soldier, a mere boy, who inquired the time of day. Upon the old gentleman innocently taking out his watch and looking at it, the soldier robbed him of it. The War was over, and this was a theft. This was all the "war experience" that the family in Columbus had.

About July 1st, Mr. Pond and I and the children moved to Walthourville and occupied Dr. Stevens' handsome summer home which he had offered us. Sam and his wife and child came up from Thomasville and also spent the summer there. It was a very large house with beautiful grounds. Captain Screven and Sister spent the summer at the plantation with Father and Mother. This was the first time they had ever spent a summer there, but our house in Jonesville had been burned. We had a very pleasant summer in Walthourville, although everybody was impoverished. Reverend Pratt Quarterman had a service for us every Sunday. Midway Church had been closed all the winter; people had no means of driving to church.

About the middle of September, our dear little daughter Cornelia, then seven years old, was taken ill with diphtheria. In spite of all that the physicians could do, she died on the first day of October, 1865. This was a great grief to us and especially to her little sister Lucy. She could read and spell and recite hymns and was a very lovable child. She had beautiful auburn hair, blue eyes, and a fair complexion, and held herself erect. My little granddaughter Eloise Slappey reminds me very much of her.

The little casket was made at the plantation, covered with white cloth, and beautiful white flowers laid upon it, and Captain Screven brought it to us to Walthourville. We laid her

little form in it, and the burial service was held at the house
of Reverend Pratt Quarterman, quite a number of our friends
being present. Then Captain Screven took the little casket
back in his double buggy to the plantation, Mr. Pond going on
horseback. They buried her in the orchard near the house, and
there she sleeps, awaiting the great resurrection. We intended
removing her remains to Laurel Grove Cemetery in Savannah
where her little sister Alice was buried, but we were unable to
do this.

I never was the same after this; it seemed to change my
whole life. Then, too, the rheumatism which had been in my
system for several years, affecting my hands and wrists, now
went into my feet also, and I became a little lame. Father was
taken very sick in October and was confined to his bed for three
months with typhoid fever. We moved back to the plantation
in November. Sam and his family went back to their home at
Cedar Hill, and Captain Screven took his family to his home
at Seabrook, finding their homes dismantled. We remained at
the plantation.

While your grandfather was still in bed, one of his negro
men, Jesse, who had begun work late in the season and who
therefore had not earned as large a share of the crop as the others, became very angry and went to Savannah and reported
your grandfather to the Freedman's Bureau established there.
The first we knew of it, he returned from Savannah accompanied by two yankee soldiers on horseback, saying they had
come to arrest my father and to take him to Savannah. As he
was unable to go, they said they would take his son. We had to
let them spend the night at our house and sit at our table.
Brother was at home on a visit, so the next day, he went with
Sam with them, also taking our faithful servant Peter to return

with Sam. They reached Savannah that afternoon and Sam was taken to the Bureau, where sat Jesse, who was first given a hearing, and Sam had to listen to his string of falsehoods. Then he was allowed to state Father's side, upon the hearing of which the presiding officer decided against Jesse, and Sam was released. To our delight, he and Peter returned safely the next day.

I must tell you of the trip your father had taken to Savannah the June before this. The yankees had not disturbed Father's cotton or his gin house, so he got your father to take three bales in a wagon with three horses, and with Peter he left for Savannah. Cousin Richard Way also went with some cotton, taking Amos with him. This was a very dangerous undertaking as they had to go through Bryan County, and the negroes there were very lawless. During the winter before, some of them had called Mr. John Pray Maxwell to his door one night and shot him dead for no reason.

They had to cross the Ogeechee River on a flat. They reached Savannah, sold their cotton, and bought what few things we had sent for (I remember calico to make Mother, Sister, myself, and the little daughters a dress, also a bolt of domestic) and left for home on the afternoon of the third day. Soon after they had left the city, they were overtaken by a squad of yankee soldiers who had been sent after them to search their wagons, saying that there had been a robbery in town the night before, and they were supposed to be the thieves. Think of it! Cousin Richard, a Presbyterian minister, and your father's character so above reproach. They had to submit to seeing their purchases opened by these miserable yankees, who finding nothing they sought, allowed them to proceed on their journey. They camped again that night at the Ogeechee and were very uneasy, as they knew they had been seen to carry cotton and were returning of course with money. Nothing disturbed them, however.

I was very anxious and as night came on, and they had not come, I became wretched, but your grandfather, always calm and hopeful, said, "If anyone can get through, Tom will; it will be all right with him." When about nine o'clock, Father, still waiting on the porch, heard the wagon and said, "Ah, there's Tom. I knew it would be all right with him." Such was his great confidence in your father's courage and ability. He made your father a present of a fine pair of boots on this trip.

This cotton brought a good price; it was sea island cotton, and from the sale of his cotton and of the rice, he got another start. He and Mr. Pond went in together and planted and made good crops, and in the spring of 1866 Father left the plantation in his care, and he and Mother went up to Athens and spent the summer with Brother, who was a Professor in the College. Your father rented a house in Jonesville, and he rode to the plantation every morning and returned every evening.

I had gotten a good cook, old Mum Rose, who had been cooking for Mother since January, so we were getting on very comfortably now. We had to become accustomed now to the new regime of paying our servants. There was a little school in the village, and we sent Lucy to it. She already could read and spell and knew her tables.

I must tell you about an old-fashioned "quilting party" I had that fall 1866. I had made with my hands during the past year a hexagon calico quilt and had sent to Savannah for the lining and border by a friend. Mother had a quilting frame, and I got Ole Chloe, who had been received back into favor, to put it in for me. I invited my friends in the village to spend the day with me and help me quilt it. I had a nice dinner, having a roast turkey, a boiled ham, fried chicken, sweet potatoes, plenty of rice, light bread and biscuits, and pickles, and macaroni and cheese, which your father had brought from Savannah on a recent trip. We were getting quite prosperous now. The ladies enjoyed the dinner very much. Then Lucy invited her little friends, and they enjoyed it too. A dinner like this was a rarity in those days.

Toward the close of this year, your grandfather Pond became quite sick, and your grandmother wrote your father an urgent letter to come to Columbus to see him and to look after his business for him. He was in his old age, the agent for the Southern Mutual Insurance Company and four others. So on the first of January, 1867, he went to Columbus and worked steadily in his father's office that month. Your grandfather recovered his health, and your father decided to move to Columbus to help him in his work. He returned to Liberty for us, and on February 26th, we left the dear old county for good.

Father made arrangements with Sam to run the plantation and in the Spring returned to Athens where he afterwards bought a nice home and "The Southern Cultivator," which he and Brother edited, and he and Mother were once more comfortable. It was arranged that we were to live at your grandfather Pond's, which we did for the rest of that year. The family were lovely to us, and we lived in great comfort. Lucy was sent to a good school, we bought nice new clothes, we had the opportunity of attending our church again, Dr. John Fulton being the rector of Trinity Church.

On the 14th of April, 1867, Palm Sunday, we had our darling little Eloise, a pretty little girl of nearly four years, baptized. Aunt Callie and I were the godmothers, and her father her godfather. She had beautiful flowing auburn curls and a fair complexion, and she wore a pale blue merino dress. Dr. Fulton took her up in his arms and kissed her after he had baptized her and gave her back to her father. Though very much frightened, she behaved beautifully. As she had been the pet of her grandparents in Liberty, now she became the pet of the family in Columbus, particularly of her grandfather, who always kept a picture of her in his drawer, as long as he lived.

Nothing of importance happened this summer, or until the morning of the 6th of October, Sunday, when we were made happy by the arrival of "another dear little daughter" as your father always said. This is the daughter who now lives with me and who is writing my reminiscences for me. This dear little baby was very pretty and healthy, and much loved by her sisters, and in fact by all the family. We named her "Anne Jones" for her Aunt Annie Pond and my maiden name. We went to housekeeping January 1st, 1868, and on my birthday, the 25th of March, a beautiful day in the church, the Feast of the Annunciation, we had little Anne Jones baptized by Dr. Fulton in Trinity Church. She was now quite pretty, and he kissed her as he returned her to her father. She was baptized in a long dress and a cap, and she also behaved beautifully, not crying a bit. Up to this time, five months, she had blue eyes; afterwards they turned brown.

Soon after this our dear Bishop Beckwith was consecrated Bishop of Georgia, and we attended the services on his first visitation to Columbus. The chancel rail was filled three times with candidates for confirmation. His eloquence held us spellbound. Soon after this, your father was made a vestryman, then treasurer, and we had a nice pew. Lucy and Ellie went to Sunday School, and we seemed to have begun life anew.

The summer of 1869, I and my three little girls spent with my father and mother in Athens. I found them very comfortable and happy, living alone in a nice, large house with large grounds, Brother and his family living not far from them. When I returned that October, I found that we had a new rector, Rev. Samuel S. Harris, Dr. Fulton having resigned in the early spring. He was a lovely man, and he and your father were bosom friends. In after years he was made Bishop of Michigan.

On the 9th of January 1870, dear Lucy was confirmed by Bishop Beckwith at night, and on the morning of the 26th of February, there came the sixth little daughter to join our family circle. In telling the news to Aunt Callie and Lucy, your father said, as he had five times before, "another dear little daughter!" This little baby was a beauty, with dark brown hair and brown eyes. We had her baptized on the 22nd of June, as your father expressed it, "on the day of her sister Alice's entrance into Paradise." Her name was "Mary Hayes" for her Aunt Mary, Sam's wife. She was baptized in the same long dress that Anne wore, and a new white cap. It was a lovely summer afternoon, and well do I remember with what pride I looked at her as her nurse brought her into the church from the vestry-room door. Her beautiful brown eyes looked all round the church as if taking in her new surroundings, and then she began to cry, never stopping until when it was all over, she was carried out. I told Mr. Harris that I felt like having it done over, but he said, "it was well done, and she had struggled hard to keep the old Adam from coming out of her, but she had not succeeded." Lucy was her young godmother and felt the responsibility to her very much, and has always been a mother to her; she calls her to this day her "sister-mother."

The November previous to this, your Aunt Margaret was

married to Dr. Theodore Starbuck of Savannah. It was a morning wedding and very quiet, only the family being present. After a nice wedding breakfast, the young couple left for Savannah, their future home.

Your grandfather Pond always had a fine vegetable garden, and frequently he would bring us a basket of nice fresh vegetables. He was a very lovable, kind, and highly educated man, and quite deaf. He had auburn hair and blue eyes; your grandmother was just the opposite with black eyes and hair. One night during the spring of this year, while your father was absent from the house attending convention, he came around after tea one night to see how we were getting on. He knocked and when we inquired from within, "Who is it?," there was no answer. He knocked again, and we said "Who is it?" again— no answer. We were becoming frightened now, fearing it was a drunken man. Finally the cook, Ann, ventured to put her head out of the front window to see, and laughingly explained, "Why it's ole Marster." He laughed heartily at our taking him for a drunken man.

We had become quite timid because one Sunday night before this, your father and I went to church, leaving Lucy at home with little Ellie and baby Anne. She was very much frightened by a drunken man coming to the house and knocking. She told him he "could not come in, Papa had the key." He went around the house, and poor little Lucy feared he had gone for an axe to break in. He said "Lemme in, lemme in!" Lucy was terrified. When we returned we were horrified to see a man lying on the front porch asleep. Your father collared him and took him out of the yard. He told your father he had mistaken the house. The cook had been left with Lucy, living in the yard, but she had gone to church too.

It was during this summer, 1870, that your father decided to apply for holy orders in the Episcopal Church. His friend Rev. John Fulton was then rector of Christ Church, Mobile, Alabama, and at his suggestion, your father decided to move to that city and take charge of a boys' school in Summerville, a suburb of Mobile, while preparing for his examination. So December 1st we bade good-by to our relatives in Columbus and moved to our new home. We occupied the rectory of St. Mary's Chapel, Summerville, and your father held lay services every Sunday. Dr. Fulton had sent out some of the rectory furniture of Christ Church (he was boarding) and hired a servant for us, so when we arrived, everything was very comfortably arranged for us.

This was a very happy period of our lives; we made many pleasant acquaintances who were very kind and generous to us. The cars ran out from Mobile all times a day, and we could go into the city whenever we wished. Lucy studied at home under her father and had many pleasant young friends. Your father and I went into the city to the exercises at the cemetery on Memorial Day, April 26th, and heard Father Ryan, the poet-priest, deliver an address to the largest crowd I have ever seen, and also in the largest cemetery. I shall never forget a beautiful drive I took with a friend on a road near the bay. I could see the vessels on the bay, in the distance, and the large magnolias on either side of the road. The plants and trees were more luxuriant than I had ever seen. The gardens in Mobile were lovely.

Your father passed his examination in May and on the 4th of June, Trinity Sunday, he was ordained deacon in Christ Church, Mobile, by Bishop Wilmer. Dr. Fulton presented him and Bishop Wilmer preached the sermon. Lucy and I were present. We had a great deal of sickness during this summer.

Every member of the family had fever but me and baby Mary. The climate agreed with me, but not with the others. During my stay in Summerville, I exchanged visits with the authoress Mrs. Augusta Evans Wilson. She had a beautiful home in Summerville, lovely large grounds and shrubbery. She was a native of Columbus, Georgia, and an old acquaintance of your father's.

On the 16th of August, your father was ordained priest, at St. Paul's Church, Spring Hill, where Bishop Wilmer lived, six miles from Mobile. The street cars ran from the city to this point, at all hours of the day. Rev. Samuel S. Harris came from Columbus to preach the ordination sermon. His text was from Acts V. 20: "Go stand and speak in the temple to the people, all the words of this life." Dr. Harris was our guest. We all went to the service; only little Mary was left behind. Dr. Nevius of St. John's Church, Mobile, presented your father. It was very solemn; the charge to the candidate was very touchingly beautiful. After it was over, we were all invited to dinner at the Bishop's. I walked from the chapel to the house, about one hundred yards, on the Bishop's arm, he in his robes.

Before this your father had received a call from St. Wilfrid's Church in Marion, Alabama, which he accepted. On August 22nd, we bade our good friends and our pleasant home good-by. We dined with our good friend Dr. Beatty, our own kind physician and his family, and took a steamer from Mobile to Selma. We enjoyed this little trip on the river very much. At Selma we took the cars from Marion, arriving there in the afternoon, Friday. We were met at the depot by two vestrymen, Captain Joe Seawell and Mr. Lee Walthall, who gave us a cordial welcome and took us to the rectory. Here we were met by Mrs. Joe Seawell, a lovely lady. The rectory was on the grounds

near the church. The ladies had furnished it and had everything in readiness for us, the beds all made, a servant engaged,
and supper ready. What a blessing this was to us weary trav-
ellers; this kindly welcome cheered us.

St. Wilfrid's was a sweet little Gothic church with stained
glass windows. Both it and the rectory had been built by the
Rev. William Stickney, who had had a large school for boys
there at one time, and had given this property to the diocese
upon his leaving. In the rear of the grounds was a large apple
orchard, and back of that was the churchyard. We found the
people very refined and hospitable. Many of them lived in
beautiful homes near the town, showing the signs of former
wealth. They would often send their carriages in for us to go
out and spend the day with them, and many were the nice presents they sent us. This was a town of colleges. There were
three, the Howard University for young men, the Judson Female Institute, and Marion Female Seminary. The president of
the latter generously offered the tuition free to our children,
and Lucy and Ellie attended it during the three years we lived
there. This was a great benefit to them. They even gave Lucy
lessons in drawing and painting, the only cost being for materials. At this writing, many of these good friends have passed
away, but I have never forgotten them or their many acts of
kindness.

The three years we lived there were comparatively happy,
but my health failed me completely. The fall of 1872, rheumatism attacked my whole system, and I was very feeble during
that winter. In May I lost the power of walking and remained
in bed for two months and a half. It was then that some of our
dear friends in the parish came to our relief, and with the help
of Bishop Wilmer, Dr. Fulton in Mobile, and my own dear fa-

ther, then living in Athens, Georgia, we were enabled to go to Hot Springs, Arkansas. The hot water from those springs is a cure for rheumatism. I could not walk, and had to be lifted often by your father in and out of trains.

We went by rail to Vicksburg, Mississippi, then took a steamer up the Mississippi River up to Memphis, having a delightful trip. We crossed the river on a flat and then took the train to Little Rock. At this place we crossed the Arkansas River, sitting in an omnibus on a flat. Here we met our kind friends, Bishop Pierce, Episcopal Bishop of Arkansas, and his wife, who took us to their house where we spent the day and night and were very kindly treated. The next morning we took the train for the Springs, but stopped at a place called Malvern, and there took a hack, passing through the roughest country I had ever seen, full of deep gorges and ravines. Your father sat by me and held me in his arms all the way, to keep me from falling. I was so very weak.

We reached the Springs in the afternoon and went to the Hot Springs Hotel. At that time, 1873, the town consisted of merely one street and houses on each side of it, and high mountains rising up on either side out of which flowed numerous springs of water, hot enough to cook an egg. From these springs, both hot and cold water were brought to the bathrooms in the hotel by means of pipes. We were very comfortably situated, and the fare was delightful, but we had to pay $80.00 a month apiece for board, $3.00 a week for baths for me, and $3.00 a week for a woman to bathe me.

For twenty-five times I was carried by porters to my bath, when I began to be able to walk feebly with my nurse. The treatment was to bathe in the hot water of a certain temperature, then to be rubbed and wrapped in blankets, and put in the dry tub, and made to drink as much hot water as I could, then taken out and rubbed down, dressed and taken back to my room. This treatment benefitted me a great deal. My physician was Dr. Lawrence, who was extremely kind and never charged us a cent for his services during our stay of two months. There was a sweet little chapel near the hotel, and Bishop Pierce asked your father to hold services in it, and told him to take the offerings, which was a help to us.

The kindness that we received on our trip there and back, and while there, showed us the great amount of goodness there is in the world. Ladies whom I had never seen nor heard of since, dressed me and combed my hair as kindly as if they had been my sisters. Your father was so lovely and sweet to me on this trip, doing all that he could and hoping for so much improvement in my health. He was obliged to return home the last of September. I was invited to stay another month as the guest of the proprietor's wife, but I could not make up my mind to let him leave me so far away, and I still so feeble. I could walk with the aid of a crutch right well, and when we reached Little Rock, I walked up the high staircase at Bishop Pierce's, up which your father had carried me two months before. If I could have remained at the Springs, I think I would have recovered my health in the process of time. But we were not able to incur any more expense. We set our faces homeward, anxious to see our dear daughters again, whom we had left at the rectory in Marion under the care of a highly esteemed maiden lady, Miss Rebecca Smith. We found them quite well when we arrived, and I thought them so pretty as they ran out to meet us, so glad to see dear Mama walking again. Lucy was a brave girl of seventeen, to stay at home with her little sisters, and let us go for so long a time. My three little girls were very pretty and sweet, and looked upon their sister like a mother. Little Anne and Mary's cheeks were like roses. Ellie was ten and had auburn curls and gray eyes, and Anne had curly light hair and brown eyes and rosy cheeks and was then six years old, and Mary was a little beauty with brown eyes and hair and rosy cheeks and was only three and a half years old.

Our dear friends welcomed us back, and we would have had a happy winter, but it was not long before I began to lose all I had gained, and on the first of March, Sunday, 1874, I stood on my feet for the last time, to try on a dress to see if it was the right length. I used to look over at the churchyard, and think I would be laid there, as there was a lot in the center of it appropriated to the rector and his family, in case, as the sexton "Crumby" said, any of them ["passed"] while they were there, but God's will was otherwise.

Cornelia Jones Pond's dictated memoir continues for a few more nearly illegible lines on page 208, which is the last page of the dictation contained in the Midway text. In 1925, Lucy T. Pond, Cornelia Jones Pond's oldest child, added fourteen pages (their numbering begins again at page 1) to bring her mother's and her family's history up to date. This section begins with comments indicating that Cornelia's narration must have gone on for a few more pages, but these are missing from the manuscript at the Midway Museum. Much of Lucy's narrative is an unembellished notation of marriages, births, and deaths, so I have summarized most of her remarks but include here her opening description of her mother's last years.

"OUR DEAR MOTHER dictated her recollections of her life this far to Anne, and said that I knew the rest and could add it if she did not, so I shall endeavor to tell of the remainder of her life, although I cannot hope to do it in the bright interesting way that she would have told it." [Signed] Lucy T. Pond

Then Lucy Pond continues:

"The visits that she spoke of to Father's parents, at Columbus, and to Uncle Sam's family, she made in the spring and summer of 1874. Father took her, Ellie, and Mary to Columbus where Uncle Sam joined them and took them to his home five miles from Thomasville, Georgia, on the Tallahassee road. He, Aunt Mary, and Lila made Mother and the children very happy and comfortable and tried to get Mother cured of rheumatism and to regain the power of walking. She did become free from pain, and her general health improved, but as was afterwards shown, she had permanently lost the ability to walk.

In August, I think it was, they all went to Athens, Ga., to visit Grandfather and Grandmother Jones, they having moved from Liberty Co. to that city as their son, Uncle Louis [William Louis Jones] lived there and was a Prof. in the University of Georgia. This was another happy visit. Aunt Rosa, who was then a widow, and her children were living with Grandfather and Grandmother, so all of the family were together, which never happened again."

As Lucy Pond reveals, in the summer of 1874, her father, Thomas Goulding Pond, was called to St. Paul's Parish in Albany, Georgia, and so after living in Alabama for four years, the family returned permanently to their home state. On October 11, 1875, Cornelia gave birth, at the age of forty-one, to the couple's only son, who was named Thomas Asa. Lucy Pond comments, "It was a great joy to them to have a son, though they were very proud of their daughters." In 1887 Mr. Pond resigned his rectorship at St. Paul's in Albany because of ill health, and the family moved to Mt. Airy, believing that the north Georgia mountain climate might help to restore him. There he took charge of the Episcopal missions at Mt. Airy, Clarksville, Tallulah Falls, Gainesville, and Toccoa. Mr. Pond died in Mt. Airy on "Easter-Even," March 24, 1894, and was buried in Oak View Cemetery in Albany, where his daughter Ellie and her husband, Robert Slappey, lived. Cornelia Jones Pond lived eight more years, residing at her home in Mt. Airy with her daughters Lucy and Anne, whose husband Henry Holcombe Bacon had died on May 12, 1897. During the last years of her life, Lucy Pond writes, Cornelia "was totally blind, from glaucoma, but her cheerfulness and Christian fortitude continued to the end, which came on May 13th, 1902." She was buried by her husband's side in Oak View Cemetery, Albany, Georgia.

APPENDIX

The Liberty County Family of Cornelia Jones Pond

ornelia Jones Pond could claim with pride, "We were related to nearly every family in the county." What follows is a listing of some of the most important of her named family connections, people whose ancestry and activities reflect Pond's sense of herself and her place in the world. Published genealogical accounts of many of Liberty County's prominent families can be found in James Stacy's *History and Records of Midway Church,* the invaluable "Who's Who" section in volume 3 of Robert Manson Myers's *The Children of Pride,* and Robert Long Groover's *Sweet Land of Liberty: A History of Liberty County, Georgia.*

The Family at Tekoah

Father, WILLIAM L. JONES. He was born in Liberty County in 1802, the fifth of eight children (three of whom died in infancy or childhood) and the third son of Samuel Jones II and Mary Way Jones (see below). His paternal grandfather, Samuel Jones I, owned extensive lands in the county by 1768. Samuel Jones I and his wife, Rebecca Baker, were married in 1763 and had four children: Rebecca, who married Robert Iverson and was the mother of Senator Alfred Iverson; Samuel II; Mary; and Sarah, who married Elias Cassels. Samuel Jones I died in 1771.

Samuel Jones I's wife, Rebecca Baker, was the daughter of William Baker Sr., first deacon of Midway Church and one of the first of the Dorchester Puritans to receive a land grant, of five hundred acres, in the Midway District in 1752. After Samuel Jones I's death, Rebecca Baker Jones married Edward Ball in 1773; widowed a second time, she married Thomas Quarterman in 1779. She died on March 15, 1792.

Samuel Jones II, born in 1767 (see Mary Way Jones, below), founded the summer retreat of Jonesville, named for his father. His sons William and Moses L. Jones, and his neighbor-kinsmen Nathaniel Varnedoe and Louis LeConte, among others, all built homes in this village and moved there during the summers. William Jones owned a plantation, Tekoah, on the South Newport River. On adjoining land was the plantation, Woodmanston, of his close friend Louis LeConte (see John and Joseph LeConte, below), with whom he shared a love of botany. With plants provided by his cousin, Alfred Iverson, William Jones successfully experimented with growing tea, and he was also a pioneer in diversified farming.

William Jones married Mary Jane Robarts in 1823, and they had six children, two of whom died in infancy. He was a Select Man for Midway Church from 1836 to 1841. With his brother Moses, he chartered a Congregational church at Jonesville. After the Civil War, he moved with his son William Louis Jones to Athens, Georgia, where they purchased and became the publishers of the *Southern Cultivator.* He died in Athens in 1885.

Mother, MARY JANE ROBARTS JONES. She was born in Liberty County in 1806, the first of three daughters of John Robarts and Elizabeth (Quarterman) (Quarterman) Robarts. Her mother, Elizabeth Quarterman, had married, first, her cousin Joseph Quarterman, with whom she had six children. One of these, Ann Quarterman, married Louis LeConte, whose plantation adjoined Tekoah and whose sons John and Joseph became famous scientists and educators (see below). Mary Jane Robarts married William Jones in 1823 and was mother to six children, four of whom survived to adulthood. She died in 1886.

Brother WILLIAM LOUIS JONES (Louis). He was born in Liberty County, Georgia, on March 27, 1827, the first son and second of six children (two daughters died in infancy) born to William and Mary Jane Robarts Jones. He grew up at Tekoah, his father's plantation, where both his father and his neighbor Louis LeConte encouraged his studies in botany. After his graduation from the University of Georgia in 1845, he took an M.D. degree at the College of Physicians and Surgeons in New York, and then, with his cousin Joseph LeConte, he studied at Harvard with the famous naturalist Louis Agassiz. In 1851 he returned to Georgia and accepted a professorship in natural science at the University of Georgia. In the same year he married Mary Williams, of Athens. He resigned his teaching position after one year, however, and began farming in Morgan County, Georgia. In 1861, on the eve of the Civil War, he returned to Athens as chair of natural science at the university. During the war, he was appointed chemist in charge of gunpowder works in Augusta. After the war he returned to the university, and in 1867 his father joined him in Athens, where they published the *Southern Cultivator*. In 1872 he became the sole editor of this prestigious agricultural journal. During the 1880s he established an agricultural studies program at the University of Georgia, finally resigning from the university in 1891. By 1886, he was writing columns on farming for Henry Grady's *Atlanta Constitution*. By 1892 he had moved to Atlanta, where he died in 1914.

Sister, ROSA JANE JONES SCREVEN. She was born in Liberty County on July 17, 1829, the oldest daughter of William and Mary Jane Robarts Jones. She grew up at Tekoah and attended private school in Macon, Georgia. In 1863, during the Civil War, she married her childhood sweetheart, Captain Benjamin Screven (1826–71), a grandson of General James Screven of Revolutionary War fame. Captain Screven was at the time of his marriage to Rosa a widower with three small boys. Serving as an officer in the Liberty Mounted Rangers, he was shot in the trachea at the battle of Hawes Shop, Virginia, in the summer of 1864. He returned to his family after the war and resumed farming, and then he joined his father-in-law's venture, publishing the *Southern Cultivator*, in Athens in 1870. Rosa and Benjamin Screven had three children in addition to his three by his first wife. After Captain Screven's death in 1871, Rosa Screven and her children lived with her father and mother in Athens.

Brother SAMUEL JOHN JONES. He was born in Liberty County on January 3, 1838, the youngest child of William and Mary Jane Robarts. He attended the University of Georgia and South Carolina Medical College, returning to Liberty County in 1858 to begin a career as a physician. He served as a nurse in a Charleston, South Carolina, military hospital during the Civil War but returned gravely ill to Tekoah, his father's plantation, shortly before Kilpatrick's Union regiment overran the county in December 1864. With Joseph Le-

Conte, he made his way out of the county in January 1865. After the war he returned to Liberty County, providing services as a physician from 1865 to 1868. He then moved to Thomasville, Georgia, where he continued his medical practice until shortly before his death in 1889. He married, first, in 1859, Mary Baxter Hayes, and second, in 1878, Mary Elizabeth Mueller. He was survived by five children.

On Neighboring Plantations and in Jonesville

Grandmother MARY WAY JONES. She was born in 1767, the daughter of Moses Way Sr. and his second wife, Ann Winn. Moses Way had come to Liberty County as a young man with his father, Parmenas Way, one of the first settlers, and he was an officer in the state troops in the Revolutionary War. Mary Way married Samuel Jones II on March 22, 1787, and they had eight children, five who lived to adulthood: Rebecca, born 1792, who married John Way; Ann, born 1794, who married Nathaniel Varnedoe; Samuel III, often listed as Samuel Jr., who married Mary E. Law; William, born 1802, who married Mary Jane Robarts; and Moses Liberty (see below), born 1805. Mary Way Jones, in later years, made her home with her youngest son, Moses Liberty Jones, at Green Forest. She died there in 1845.

Uncle MOSES L. JONES. He was born in Liberty County in 1805, the youngest son of Samuel Jones II and Mary Way Jones. He owned and farmed Green Forest, one of the largest plantations in Liberty County. He was a Select Man for Midway Church from 1842 until his death in 1851, and with his brother William, he chartered a Congregational church in Jonesville, Georgia, where he had a summer home. He married Saccarissa Elizabeth Axson, daughter of Dr. Samuel Jacob Axson and Ann Lambright (Dicks), on November 18, 1830. They had nine children, eight of whom lived to adulthood. His daughter Eugenia Jones (Bacon) wrote a novel, *Lyddy: A*

Tale of the Old South, published in 1898, based on her family's life at Green Forest. Saccarissa Axson Jones died from complications connected to the birth of her last son, Clifford Jones, on October 31, 1850. Moses L. Jones died on May 28, 1851, leaving eight children. His brother William became the administrator of his estate.

Cousin LAURA CLIFFORD JONES (CAMP). She was born in Liberty County in 1832, the oldest child of Moses L. and Saccarissa Axson Jones. She grew up at Green Forest and in Jonesville. When she was nineteen years old, after her father's death in 1851, she became the guardian of her seven siblings. In 1859 she married Raleigh Spinks Camp, who attained the rank of major during the Civil War and commanded Confederate forces at the siege of Vicksburg. After the Civil War Major and Laura Jones Camp moved to Atlanta with their two children. Raleigh Spinks Camp died there in 1867. Laura Jones Camp died in 1911 in Birmingham, Alabama, where she lived with her son, Augustus Jones Camp.

Cousin LEONORA JONES (MCCONNELL) (STACY). She was born in Liberty County in 1838, the second daughter and third of nine children of Moses L. and Saccarissa Axson Jones. In 1857 she married Thomas Rush McConnell. Her husband died suddenly in Mobile, Alabama, in April 1861, shortly after receiving his commission in the Confederate army. Leonora Jones McConnell returned to Liberty County to live with her sister Laura Jones Camp for the duration of the war. She became the second wife of Dr. Robert Quarterman Stacy in 1866 and moved with him first to Atlanta and then to New York City, where he practiced medicine until his death in 1882.

Cousin MARY LOUISA JONES (BACON). She was born in 1819 in Liberty County, the only daughter of Mary E. Law Jones and her husband, Samuel Jones III, who died in the year that Louisa was born. Samuel Jones III was the oldest son of Samuel Jones II and

Mary Way Jones. Louisa Jones married the Reverend Augustus O. Bacon, son of Thomas and Sarah Holcombe Bacon, and died at the age of twenty-one in 1840, leaving a one-year-old son, Augustus O. Bacon Jr. (born October 20, 1839), and a three-year-old son, Samuel Jones Bacon, who died October 6, 1840, and who is buried with her in Midway Cemetery. Augustus O. Bacon Jr. grew up in Liberty County and Savannah, Georgia, served in the Confederate army, and after the war became an important leader of the Democratic Party in Georgia. He was elected to the United States Senate four times, beginning in 1894 and serving until his death in 1914. Bacon County, in Georgia, is named for him.

Cousin RICHARD QUARTERMAN WAY. Richard Quarterman Way was born in Liberty County in 1819, the son of John Way Jr. and Rebecca Jones Way (born 1792). His father was the son of John Way Sr. and Jemima Quarterman (daughter of John Quarterman Sr.). His mother, Rebecca, was the oldest child of Samuel Jones II and Mary Way Jones. He attended Franklin College and Columbia Seminary and became a Presbyterian minister in 1843. In that year he married Susan Quarterman, daughter of the Reverend Robert Quarterman (see below). Richard and Susan Way sailed that year for China, where they served as missionaries for sixteen years, returning to Liberty County in 1858 with their six children. From 1859 to 1866, Richard Way served as preacher to Liberty County slaves through the support of Midway Church. In 1886 he moved to Savannah, where he was minister to the Anderson Street (Second) Presbyterian Church. Susan Way died in Savannah in 1893, and Richard Quarterman died there in 1895.

Cousin SAMUEL MCWHIR VARNEDOE (Ole Mac). He was born in Liberty County in 1816, the son of Nathaniel Varnedoe and Ann Jones Varnedoe, daughter of Samuel Jones II and Mary Way Jones. He graduated from Franklin College in 1836 and returned home to teach at the school founded by his kinsmen in Jonesville, Georgia. He was named for another famous Liberty County teacher, Dr. William McWhir. Both men were known for their harsh discipline. In 1866 Samuel McWhir Varnedoe established Valdosta Institute, a school that he served until his death in 1878.

Cousins JOHN AND JOSEPH LECONTE. They were sons of Louis LeConte (1782–1838) and Ann Quarterman LeConte (1793–1826) and grew up on their father's plantation, Woodmanston. Their father was a famous botanist whose gardens at Woodmanston were a nationally acclaimed showplace between 1826 and 1839. Their mother, Ann Quarterman, was the daughter of Elizabeth Quarterman and her first husband, Joseph Quarterman, and so she was half sister to Mary Jane Robarts Jones, whose husband, William Jones, owned Tekoah, a plantation that shared borders with Woodmanston. Louis and Ann LeConte had six children, among them Jane, born 1814, who married Dr. J. M. B. Harden, and Ann, born in 1825, who married Dr. J. P. Stevens.

John LeConte, born 1818, graduated from Franklin College and the College of Physicians and Surgeons in New York and taught physics and mathematics at both of these schools. In 1856 he accepted a professorship at South Carolina College in Columbia, where he remained until the outbreak of the Civil War. In 1841 he married Josephine Graham, a celebrated beauty whose popularity with the students at Franklin College is said to have infuriated the wife of its president, Alonzo Church.

Joseph LeConte, born 1823, followed the path of his elder brother John, studying at Franklin College and the College of Physicians and Surgeons. In 1847 he married Elizabeth Nisbet, and the following year he began a medical practice in Macon, Georgia. Two years later he moved his young family to the North, where, with his cousin William Louis Jones, he studied geology and zoology at Harvard University with the famous professor Louis Agassiz, a friend of his father's. He returned to Georgia to join his brother on the faculty of the University of Georgia in 1852 and then went with him to South Carolina College in 1856, accepting a professorship in geology and chemistry.

Both John and Joseph LeConte served the Confederacy during the Civil War; Joseph's account of his adventures through enemy lines to Liberty County in December 1864, when he went there to rescue his sisters and daughter, was published in 1937 as *Ware Sherman*. John and Joseph LeConte moved to Berkeley, California, in 1869, accepting posts at the newly created University of California. John served as its president from 1876 to 1881; Joseph was an acclaimed professor of geology and natural history there from 1869 to 1896. John LeConte died in Berkeley in 1891; Joseph died there in 1901. Joseph's daughter, Emma LeConte Furman, wrote an account of her father's activities and Sherman's burning of Columbia, entitled *When the World Ended*, which was published in 1957.

At Midway Church

Uncle ROBERT QUARTERMAN. The Reverend Robert Quarterman was born in 1787, son of Thomas Quarterman and his third wife, the twice-widowed Rebecca Baker. His mother's first husband was Samuel Jones I, so Robert Quarterman was the half brother of Samuel Jones II. Robert Quarterman was ordained minister of Midway Church in 1823 and held that post until 1847. He was the first pastor of Midway Church to be born in the county and raised as a member of the church. He was married four times and had twelve children. Five of his sons, including Nathaniel Pratt Quarterman (1839–1915), became Presbyterian ministers. Robert Quarterman died in 1849 and was buried in Midway Cemetery.

ISAAC STOCKTON KEITH AXSON. The Reverend Axson was born in Charleston, South Carolina, in 1813. He became co-pastor, with Robert Quarterman, of Midway Church in 1836 and also served

Jonesville Church. He remained pastor of Midway Church until 1853 and then became president of Greensboro Female College in Greensboro, Georgia. His sister Saccarissa Axson was married to Moses L. Jones; two of their daughters, Leonora Jones Stacy and Eugenia Jones Bacon, attended Greensboro Female College during his presidency. In 1857 the Reverend Axson was called to Independent Presbyterian Church, Savannah, where he served until his death in 1891. On June 24, 1885, he officiated, in Independent Presbyterian Church, at the wedding of his granddaughter, Ellen Louise Axson, and Thomas Woodrow Wilson, later the twenty-eighth president of the United States. On July 14, 1853, he had officiated, in William Jones's home in Jonesville, Georgia, at the wedding of Cornelia Jones and Thomas Goulding Pond.

The Goulding/Pond Family

Husband, THOMAS GOULDING POND. He was born in Lexington, Georgia, on January 31, 1827, the son of Thomas Asa and Lucy Anne Goulding Pond. He grew up in Columbus, Georgia, and graduated from Franklin College, with second honors, in 1845. He married Cornelia Jones in 1853. In that year he resigned his position at Franklin College and became professor of mathematics at Tuskegee Female College. After a year there, he accepted, in 1854, a professorship in mathematics at Chatham Academy in Savannah. He held several posts in the Confederate army, including an officership in the Liberty Mounted Rangers, and served during the last months of the war under General Wade Hampton in Virginia and South Carolina. After the war he studied for the ministry and was ordained in the Episcopal Church. He served as pastor of several Alabama churches before accepting a call to St. Paul's in Albany, Georgia, in 1874. In 1887, for health reasons, he moved with his family to Mt. Airy, where he supervised several mission churches in the mountains of northeast Georgia. He died in Mt. Airy in 1894 and is buried in Albany, Georgia.

Father and mother-in-law, THOMAS ASA AND LUCY GOULDING POND. Lucy Goulding Pond, the mother of Thomas Goulding Pond, was born in Liberty County, the daughter of the Reverend Thomas and Ann Holbrook Goulding. Lucy's father, the Reverend Thomas Goulding, was born in 1786 to Thomas Goulding and Margaret Stacy Goulding. He was the first native-born Presbyterian minister of Liberty County and taught school at Sunbury and in McIntosh County before being ordained pastor of White Bluff Church, near Savannah, in 1816. In 1822 he was called to a church in Lexington, Georgia. Thomas Asa and Lucy Pond lived in Lexington for a brief time after their marriage but moved to Columbus, Georgia, where he became an insurance agent after the Civil War. Thomas Asa Pond died in 1882.

Uncle FRANCIS ROBERT GOULDING. He was born in Liberty County in 1810, the son of the Reverend Thomas Goulding and Ann Holbrook Goulding. He graduated from Franklin College and Columbus Theological Seminary and was pastor of the Presbyterian church in Darien, Georgia, from 1856 to 1862. He served as a chaplain in the Confederate army and after the war moved to Roswell, Georgia, where he died in 1881. His juvenile book, *Robert and Harold; or the Young Marooners on the Florida Coast* (1852), achieved international fame.

> The Children of Thomas Goulding Pond
> (1827–94) and Cornelia Jones Pond
> (1834–1902) [The marriage dates of
> the Pond children are contained in
> Lucy Pond's addendum to her mother's
> journal, dated 1925.]

Lucy Tallulah, born April 13, 1856, in Savannah, Georgia.
Mary Cornelia, born February 20, 1858, in Savannah, Georgia. She
    died October 1, 18 65, of diphtheria, in Walthourville, Georgia.

Alice Goulding, born August 26, 1860, in Savannah, Georgia. She died June 22, 1861, of scarlet fever, in Savannah.

Eloise Thomas, born June 3, 1863, at Tekoah in Liberty County, Georgia. She married Robert Slappey on November 4, 1886.

Anne Jones, born October 6, 1867, in Columbus, Georgia. She married, first, Henry Holcombe Bacon, on January 9, 1889. He died in 1897; she married, second, the Rev. William Henry Zeigler, a Presbyterian minister, on August 18, 1904.

Mary Hayes, born June 22, 1870, in Columbus, Georgia. On June 24, 1891, she married her cousin, Dr. George Orville Jones Sr., who died in 1924.

Thomas Asa, born October 11, 1875, in Albany, Georgia. On April 11, 1905, he married Katherine Creswell West.